PRAISE FOR LOVE REVEALS THE HEART OF GOD

"To describe this book in four words, I would say: awesome, inspiring, reviving and eye-opening. *Love Reveals The Heart of God* is penned by a dedicated and inspired man of God who is used by God to reveal himself to others through this text. In this text, Reverend Merits Henry has proven that we can have real intimacy with God, our spouses, family and others when we seek to remain shadowed in the heart of God in God's Love. Simultaneously touching spiritual and social relationships, this work of art speaks to concerns that have for too long been neglected by both the spiritual and secular world. *Love Reveals The Heart of God* is profoundly filled with extraordinary discerned, inspired and revealed words that are powerful enough to touch and change hearts for as long as it is read. The reader will be liberated simply because the author relates a universal real life situation, that of Love, which is contextualized in all aspects to bring out the divine–God's purpose for our lives."

—Estella Wheeler

Thank You!
This is your heart
a new beginning
M Henry

MERITS R. HENRY

Love Reveals the HEART OF GOD

HAVING INTIMACY WITH GOD
THROUGH CHRIST IS ALL THAT MATTERS

Love Reveals the
HEART OF GOD

LOVE REVEALS THE HEART OF GOD
Copyright © 2014 by Merits R. Henry

Scripture quotations marked KJV are taken from the Holy Bible, King James Version, which is in the public domain. Scripture quotations marked NKJV taken from the New King James Version®. Copyright © 1982 by Thomas Nelson, Inc. Used by permission. All rights reserved. Scripture quotations marked NIV are taken from the Holy Bible, NEW INTERNATIONAL VERSION®. Copyright © 1973, 1978, 1984, 2011 by Biblica, Inc. All rights reserved worldwide. Used by permission. NEW INTERNATIONAL VERSION® and NIV® are registered trademarks of Biblica, Inc. Use of either trademark for the offering of goods or services requires the prior written consent of Biblica US, Inc. Scripture quotations marked NASB are taken from the New American Standard Bible®, Copyright © 1960, 1962, 1963, 1968, 1971, 1972, 1973, 1975, 1977, 1995 by The Lockman Foundation. Used by permission. Scripture quotations are taken from the Holy Bible, New Living Translation, copyright ©1996, 2004, 2007 by Tyndale House Foundation. Used by permission of Tyndale House Publishers, Inc., Carol Stream, Illinois 60188. All rights reserved. Scripture quotations marked JUB are taken from The Jubilee Bible (from the Scriptures of the Reformation) edited by Russell M. Stendal Copyright © 2000, 2001, 2010 May be quoted in other works. May be used freely in all non-profit, non-commercial Bible distribution endeavors provided the content is not altered. For all commercial reproduction, express written permission from the publisher is required. First edition published 2000. Scripture quotations marked ESV are from The Holy Bible, English Standard Version® (ESV®), copyright © 2001 by Crossway, a publishing ministry of Good News Publishers. Used by permission. All rights reserved. Scriptures marked MSG are taken from The Message. Copyright © by Eugene H. Peterson 1993, 1994, 1995, 1996, 2000, 2001, 2002. Used by permission of NavPress Publishing Group. Scriptures marked NLT are taken from the HOLY BIBLE, NEW LIVING TRANSLATION (NLT) Copyright© 1996, 2004, 2007 by Tyndale House Foundation. Used by permission of Tyndale House Publishers, Inc., Carol Stream, Illinois 60188. All rights reserved. Used by permission. Scriptures marked TLB are taken from the THE LIVING BIBLE (TLB): Scripture taken from THE LIVING BIBLE copyright© 1971. Used by permission of Tyndale House Publishers, Inc., Carol Stream, Illinois 60188. All rights reserved. Scriptures marked ISV are taken from the INTERNATIONAL STANDARD VERSION, copyright© 1996-2008 by the ISV Foundation. All rights reserved internationally. Scriptures marked NCV are taken from the NEW CENTURY VERSION (NCV): Scripture taken from the NEW CENTURY VERSION®. Copyright© 2005 by Thomas Nelson, Inc. Used by permission. All rights reserved. Scriptures marked NLV are taken from the New Life Version, Copyright 1969, 1976, 1978, 1983, 1986, Christian Literature International, P. O. Box 777, Canby, OR 97013. Used by permission. Scriptures marked ERV are taken from the HOLY BIBLE: EASY-TO-READ VERSION © 2001 by Bible League International. and used by permission. Scriptures marked GWT are taken from GOD'S WORD®, © 1995 God's Word to the Nations. Used by permission of Baker Publishing Group. Scriptures marked AKJV are taken from the American King James Version which is in the public domain.

Printed In Canada

ISBN: 978-1-4866-0541-5

Word Alive Press
131 Cordite Road, Winnipeg, MB R3W 1S1
www.wordalivepress.ca

MIX
Paper from
responsible sources
FSC® C016245

Cataloguing in Publication may be obtained through Library and Archives Canada

If people can learn to hate, they can be taught to love.
                                                —Nelson Mandela

Jesus on earth high over all, in earth and hell and sky;
Angels and man before me fall while devils fear and fly!
                                                —Amy Woodhouse

Contents

DESIGNED EMOTIONALLY. . . CREATED PHYSICALLY . . .

For you created my inmost being; you knit me together in my mother's womb.

I praise you because I am fearfully and wonderfully made; your works are wonderful, I know that fully well.

My frame was not hidden from you when I was made in the secret place, when I was woven together in the depths of the earth
—Psalm 139: 13–15, NIV

A Prayer Of Love
BY THE APOSTLE PAUL

I pray that out of his glorious riches he may strengthen you with power through his Spirit in your inner being, so that Christ may dwell in your hearts through faith. And I pray that you, being rooted and established in love, may have power, together with all the Lord's holy people, to grasp how wide and long and high and deep is the love of Christ, and to know this love that surpasses knowledge—that you may be filled to the measure of all the fullness of God
—Ephesians 3: 16–19, NIV

Dedication

This book is for everyone who has a desire and hunger for a deeper revelation of the heart of God. Yes, you have been longing and praying for true understanding of the Lord. But for those who have followed the traditions of religions, rituals, customs, traditions, and works, you will discover that there is only one way to truly understand and come to the knowledge of God, and that is by studying His word, through an intimate desire with fasting and prayer, and by continually seeking the face of the Lord.

To those who are experiencing the overflowing of God's Love and who are willing to share with the world the Love of God and to tell of His grace and mercy, this book will inspire you to find great joy in doing so, and it will encourage you to lead others to the Lord.

To the millions of believers who are enjoying the Love of God, and to those who are struggling with unforgiveness, you will find the joy and the peace which you so desire in reading this book. Please know also, that there is a 'peace that passes all understanding' and one can only find this peace through the genuine Love of God.

You can only experience this Love of God when you believe and trust in Him . This experience will completely transform your life. May you find peace through the Love of God, and may the generation to follow find joy through the genuine Love of Almighty God.

Acknowledgements

There is no better gift than the gift of Love

Nothing in life can ever be successful without the cooperative effort of gifted and talented people who are willing to share their talents and ideas, and to make genuine sacrifice and commitments by offering their experiences and their passion for the common goal of the success of others. I am always reminded that we are the sum total of the people whom we have met,[1] those who have taught us to believe in ourselves, regardless of the obstacles that we may confront. Those people willingly share their experiences with us, thus allowing us to learn from them. This work is the product of godly and precious individuals whose thoughts, ideas and hard work have given me the exposure and the inspiration which have enhanced my understanding of the writing process, thus equipping me with the courage that empowered me to embark on my journey as a writer. Through the grace and through the inspiration of Almighty God and through the guidance of the Holy Spirit, with the help of these individuals, I was able to complete this book.

I want to acknowledge Elder Cecil and Mary Givans for their support and deep affirmation of Love given in time of greatest need. Thanks to everyone who participated. Without your effort and support, this project would not have been completed.

---

1   Myles Munroe, "Rediscovering the Kingdom" (Shippensburg, PA: Destiny Image Publishers, Inc., 2004), 12.

I extend a heart of gratitude to my editorial advisors whose insight, contribution, encouragement and kind thoughts have helped to make this book possible. With a heart of gratitude, I would like to extend special thanks to Ms. Earlena Dawson. Your in-depth thoughts and refining suggestions are the excellent content of this book.

Thank you to Mr. Albert Hall. Your sincere conviction inspires the dreams of this book, above and beyond.

Many thanks to the 'Promise' I discovered through the heart of God's Love. You have demonstrated the virtue of being patient and understanding during my communion with the heart of God and during my late night writing. Thank you for demonstrating God's gracious Love and faithfulness to me each day of my life. My achievements are also your success.

To my precious children, you fill my heart each day with Love. You are the greatest gifts given to me from the Lord.

With my whole heart, I thank you, Lord. Thank you, Lord, for allowing me to develop and refine these ideas and concepts; you are indeed the Lover who has no end. Your Love sustains me and leaves me with an awesome feeling of gratitude and thankfulness. Thank You, Lord.

DAILY LOVE THOUGHTS

May the flame of God's words ignite the fire of Love in your heart!

DAY ONE: MY THOUGHTS TO YOU

The Love of God is real and is unlike any other Love; this eternal Love is for everyone to receive because it is freely given. The beauty of Jesus' Love is that it is able to transform every area of our life. After spending many years as a Christian, I now understand the beauty of Christ's Love within me. For me, this is the blessed hope that I live for: to abide in the beauty of God's Love, where I can believe and feel that I am growing in the wisdom and knowledge of His Love and of His grace. This has been a lifelong dream for me to attain the highest point in my Christian walk with the Lord, where I am now feeling secure, nurtured and nourished in the divine Love of God.

MEMORY VERSE:

Surely your goodness and unfailing Love will pursue me all the days of my life, and I will live in the house of the LORD forever
—Psalm 23:6, NLT

DAY TWO: MY THOUGHTS TO YOU

Do not be deceived like Eve, in the Garden of Eden. Fairytale promises are fantasies devised by the enemy to entrap Christian believers. Believers must understand that the Love of Christ Jesus is real. Jesus is the believer's only hope; therefore, always look to Jesus, believe in His Love, knowing that He is your 'Alpha and your Omega.'

MEMORY VERSE:

In order that Satan might not outwit [outsmart] us. For we are not unaware of his schemes
—2 Corinthians 2:11, NIV

DAY THREE: MY THOUGHTS TO YOU

Love is the transforming agent of your spirit; it defines your beauty from within, it changes your relationships and character. Love keeps the best secrets of your heart and it has the ability to change your darkest thoughts.

Memory Verse:

For it is God who works in you to will and to act in order to fulfill his good purpose

—Philippians 2:13, NIV

DAY FOUR: MY THOUGHTS TO YOU

Your relationship with God is sealed with Love; this reveals the perfect beauty in you. This beauty is pure and it cannot be hidden. It shines in darkness and it also stands out everywhere you go, and it brings you unlimited favors and everlasting blessings.

MEMORY VERSE:

It is the blessing of the LORD that makes rich, And He adds no sorrow to it

—Proverbs 10:22, NASB

DAY FIVE: MY THOUGHTS TO YOU

You are beautifully created and you are eternally Loved by God. With His precious eyes, He watches over you and your family; He assigned His angels to guard you, as He had assigned angels and shepherds to protect and to watch over Joseph and Mary at the birth of their son Jesus. The Lord will work out all situations in your favor and for your own good. But it is incumbent upon you to seize the opportunities that are set before you; there is no need for you to be continuously struggling with negative thoughts and negative self-image, for the Lord is in control of all of your situations.

Memory Verse:

He shall cover thee with his feathers, and under his wings shalt thou trust: his truth shall be thy shield and buckler

—Psalm 91:4, KJV

DAY SIX: MY THOUGHTS TO YOU

In the eyes of the Lord, you are precious. You were ideally selected and created in God's own image to accomplish His divine will. Whenever you are struggling with self-identity, remember, that the Love of God teaches you how to Love and how to accept and appreciate yourself. However, the first step is for you to truthfully examine and evaluate yourself before God, then take the first step in evaluating your experience, your wholeness and your freedom with God; as you acknowledge your deficiencies in Him , you will then be able to obtain your redemption through the inspiration and guidance of the Holy Spirit. Once you have fully accepted and believe that you are divinely created and that you are graciously Loved by the Lord, then it will become much easier for you to accept who you really are: a Child of God, walking in His promises through His Love

Memory Verse:

He performs wonders that cannot be fathomed, miracles that cannot be counted

—Job 5:9, NIV

DAY SEVEN: MY THOUGHTS TO YOU

Be comforted through all your situations: regardless of the situation, remember that God is in control of your life, if only you put your trust in Him . He has a plan for everything and for every situation concerning you. You may not know what your future holds, but give thanks unto the Lord and rest assured that He holds your future in His hands. God's Love is limitless and His grace is measureless; He is omnipotent, omniscient and omnipresent. Through His son, Jesus Christ, His grace is given to you without measure. Never forget that you were created in His likeness; therefore, put your trust in the Lord, and He will keep you in His abounding Love; and above all, rejoice in the Lord; and again I say rejoice!

Memory Verse:

May your unfailing Love be my comfort, according to your promise to your servant
—Psalm 119:76, NIV

DAY EIGHT: MY THOUGHTS TO YOU

Those of you who are involved in any relationship must find ways in which to create the means of establishing genuine compatibility so that the relationship may remain stable. A relationship should not be built on words alone, but it should also be built on honesty and trust, and should be governed by the genuine Love of God. This is the kind of relationship that goes beyond the physical realm of human understanding because it is governed by the true and only *Love which is revealed from the heart of God – agape Love!*

Memory Verse:

Two people can accomplish more than twice as much as one; they get a better return for their labor. If one person falls, the other can reach out and help. But people who are alone when they fall are in real trouble. And on a cold night, two under the same blanket can gain warmth from each other…
—Ecclesiastes 4: 9 – 11, NLT

DAY NINE: MY THOUGHTS TO YOU

The future of a believer is already planned and laid out by the Lord before he is conceived. You, the believer in Christ, are made and prepared for the mission ordained for you by the Lord. Therefore it is the Lord's will to bring out that which He has placed within you so that others may see the beauty of the Lord shining through you and come to glorify Him .

Merits R. Henry

Memory Verse:

And I am sure that God who began the good work within you will
keep right on helping you grow in his grace until his task within you
is finally finished on that day when Jesus Christ returns
                                                    —Philippians 1: 6, TLB

Foreword

GOD'S LOVE FOR MANKIND.

The Lord created the family unit as a reflection of his Love for humanity

When God created the earthly family, He meant it to be a reflection of His own image on earth, through which His Love would be manifested. It is through this institution of lifelong covenant with the earthly family that God, in His wisdom, created the man and the woman and personally named the man Adam: "*And the Lord formed man of the dust and of the ground and breathed into his nostrils the breath of life; and man became a living soul...*" (Genesis 2:7, KJV); "*And the rib which the Lord God had taken from the man, made he a woman...*" (Genesis 2:22, KJV). After creation, God instructed 'Adam' that both he and his wife, whom Adam named Eve, should: "*Be fruitful*" (Genesis 1:28, KJV) and God blessed them.

In the hierarchy of the family structure, the father stands as the most important link between his family and the Heavenly Father; just as Jesus was given the responsibility by His Father, to demonstrate the Love of the Father to the world, through those whom His Father had given into His care. So too God empowered the first earthly father, Adam, with the responsibility of the family, through which the world should come to accept and embrace the Love of God. Jesus declared: "*I have manifested thy name unto the men which thou gavest me out of the world...and they have kept thy word*" (John 17:6, KJV). Jesus led by example as His life on earth exemplified the plan of God for the new covenant.

The commission was given to Jesus by His Heavenly Father to establish His Kingdom on earth; so too was the command given to the earthly father, Adam, as head of the first family. Jesus served as the ultimate example of obedience and holy righteous living which are the greatest responsibilities. This gives Jesus the right to stand as the High Priest between the family unit and between God and the family. The expectation was that Adam should demonstrate the Love and the righteousness of God through his obedience to God's instructions. It was by these exemplary attributes, through the godly life of the earthly family that the world would have come to know, acknowledge and glorify the Lord. Adam failed, but the grace of God abides through Jesus Christ, whom God appointed to take over responsibility through His death on the cross, to redeem mankind back unto Himself. Jesus was always in constant prayer with and for those whom His Father had given into His care. He stated: *"I pray for them... which thou hast given me...those that thou gave to me I have kept,"* (John 17:9,12, KJV). Thus, today, because of the nurturing care that Jesus exhibited to those who were entrusted to Him by His Father, many have now come to know, acknowledge and understand the blessedness and the hope of the glorious redemption, and the joyous promises of eternal life, with the Heavenly Father, through Jesus Christ the Son.

Through *Love Reveals the Heart of God*, Merits' aim is to uncover the Love of God so that all can see and experience the vastness of God's Love. He brings out fresh revelation that defines the value of Love, as well as the promises which are wrapped up in the Lord's Love. He has also given us meaningful reference notes and detailed perspectives on Love through the eyes of God. Additionally, he reveals sound principles on Love for families, along with essential, corporate, and personal life lessons. Merits focuses on the believers in Christ and the unbelievers who desire to understand the measureless Love of Christ.

This book is practical for everyday life. It also gives objective references that focus primarily on family values; it is filled with instructions concerning the fruit of Love and the family structure, such as understanding of the family, maturity of the family, singleness of the mind, marriage, widowhood, and other family issues.

In *Love Reveals the Heart of God*, Merits' gives us not just his personal recommendations, but he also recommends to us the tranquillity of the Holy Spirit. Many writers have written about the Love of God;

however, few have unearth the true meaning of God's Love as Merits has cleverly done.

To everyone who has been searching and praying for a deeper meaning of the Lord's unmerited Love, this book reveals to you within each page 'THE VOICE OF GOD.' Merits also provides the source of hope to his readers.

—Earlena Dawson
Director of Arts and Science
B.A.Eng. Hon.Edu.

Preface

We can also be taught how to Love one another

Because of the many perils which exist in our world, the church is obligated to take action and become a more caring community in its attempt to win souls for the Kingdom of God. The purpose of this immediate command is to spread the good news of the Love of God so that the world may see and experience the heart of our Lord Jesus as King. The devourer is continuously trying to spread hatred and create chaos in an attempt to destroy and prevent people from truly experiencing the heart of God.

Therefore, as the church examines as well as establishes models, patterns and other eschatological approaches, it must of course provide "unshackling aids" to a world that is unaware of the everlasting Love of God. As the church endeavors to take on the responsibility of spreading the gospel of Christ, it must equip itself with the knowledge and with the power of God. (See Proverb 29:18 and Colossian 1:19.) Also, the church must endeavor to demonstrate both the earthly and heavenly wisdom of Solomon. These things can only be accomplished by trusting and believing in Jesus Christ, and by studying and following the Word of the Lord. There must be an understanding that Jesus is Lord of our lives and everything in life must be microscopically viewed in the light of His lordship. Even though Solomon was highly gifted with wisdom, in his role as king, he had still fallen into idolatry. Therefore, it should not be forgotten that, according to 1 Corinthians 1:21, the world cannot function on its worldly knowledge, it must recognize the Lord is in charge, therefore it can only function through the wisdom and knowledge of God. We are not doubtful that Solomon's wisdom was a gift and a blessing given to him by the Lord.

The church must manifest the characteristics of the Lord Jesus. Its role should be evident and identifiable within each community. To be effective in winning souls, the Spirit of Love has to be personally sown in the soil of each member's heart. This should begin with education of the church family of the appropriate life lessons necessary in order to understand God's commission. Becoming a worker, worshipper, and warrior of the Word of God are of paramount importance if we are determined to reach the world with the Love of Christ. The proper approach to mentoring includes:

- Embracing the parable of Luke 15 which teaches us that lost people matter most to God, therefore, they should matter to us as well;
- Seeing programs or communities as a mission field ministry, sowing seeds in anticipation of the harvest which constitutes our survival, for without the harvest, we perish;
- Looking at that community with the eyes of Love, since the functioning of every part of the body of Christ is to cause growth to the body and to edify itself in Love. (See Ephesians 4:11–16.) Without the completion of the body, we are incomplete.

If the church is able to develop and maintain this concept by understanding its divine assignment wrapped in John 3:16 that God so Loved the world, then it will be better able to reach the world with the gospel of Christ. The most crucial part of the church's development, should be Love. We must also understand that Love is the tool of enlistment, evangelism, world mission, equipping of the saints, and it is also the means by which new converts are drawn to the family of God.

Jesus intended for us to have the same connection of assignments and power as he had with His Father.[11] Christian leaders today generally inform the world about Christ; however, some of these leaders have purposefully

---

II J.R. Allebach, Church Planting Handbook, "Gospel Crusade Ministerial Fellowship" (GCMF Publishing, 2004),57

taken the Lord off His throne and have replaced Him with their brand of doctrine. How do they do this? one may ask. They do so by setting the standards by which believers should and must enter into eternal life, thus ostracizing many who have the desire to gain eternal life through Jesus Christ. They must remember, though, that they are not God; they are only the medium through which the Lord spread His Love. Therefore, instead of just informing others about the Lord, our lives and actions must radiate the Love and the power of Jesus Christ. Acts 10:38 reveals that Jesus *"went about doing good"* (Acts 10:38, NIV) by showing Love and mercy; for this reason, the people followed Him. He taught them the truth about salvation, and in so doing, He taught them how to Love one another; He showed them compassion by healing their diseases. These examples of Jesus demonstrate to Christian leaders that they must forfeit their one-dimensional approach to soul winning and empower themselves to serve one another as they encourage and support one another in Love.

If the church must represent the Lord to the world, it has to adorn itself with the characteristics of Jesus Christ. (See Ephesians 4:17–32; Colossians 3:11–17; 2 Corinthians 4:16–18; 1 Peter 3:3–4; Psalm 119:97–98; John 17:13–19 and Matthew 5:13–20.) According to Augustine, "The church must be a fellowship of Love, patterned after an orderly universe, exhibiting order and structure."[III]

Humanity has tried to develop an ecclesiology to govern the church and its mission but there is no answer apart from salvation. (*Mastering Pastoral Counseling Utilizing Temperament,* Luton, Arno, and Arno, 1997)

Biblical scholars have expressed thoughts and theories of Christ and the church. According to the National Christian Counseling Association (NCCA), Eric G. Jay says, "Augustine saw the church of Christ apart from which there is no Salvation, while Martin Luther saw the church as the congregation of saints invisibly known to God."[IV] Even though these scholars demonstrate a valid awareness of God and Christianity, there are certain important elements that are missing due to their over-simplified theories.

III   Mastering Pastoral Counseling Utilizing Temperament, 4th ed.,(APS), Richard G. Arno and Phyllis J. Arno (National Christian Counseling Association, Florida, 1997), 42

IV Ibid, 35

They attempt to capture the concept of the church as it relates to the spreading of the gospel. Nevertheless, they fail to grasp the concept of the true purpose of the church, which is to serve its community with Love. Sadly, many of today's churches still portray elements of these flawed approaches.

Deep Bible truth reveals that God sacrifices His Love to save the lost. A decision was made at Calvary to extend God's Love to humanity. After the death, burial and resurrection of Jesus, God's Love through the shed blood of Jesus gives hope, assurance and access to the throne of GOD to everyone regardless of their culture, previous beliefs or doctrines. Thus by this decision, we all benefit from the Love of Jesus.

Throughout the ages, God has been revealing His characteristics to us throughout the Scriptures. One of the ways He reveals Himself to us is through the questions He asks, such as was asked of Peter and even of Job during his suffering, "Who do men say that I am?" Considering these questions from a more spiritual background, shows that God uses questions as a device to communicate His plans to us. Furthermore, this shows also that God is teaching us something about His nature and character— Love. I believe He is leading us into the "secrets" of His heart.

As agents of change to proclaim His Kingdom, God wants to perform within us, His parenting role which is His Love! This has to be accomplished before we can understand who he really is. Love ultimately establishes the grand partnership with Jesus within our hearts. The Lord has chosen to reach the world through us, meaning that we are God's instruments on the earth. (See Ephesians 2:10 and 1 Corinthians 3:9.) We have always been in the plan of God; for this reason He makes His appeal of Love and reconciliation to the world through us. (See 2 Corinthians 5:20.)

From this mystery, it is evident that God, the omniscient savior, has never limited Himself to perform His work. Nevertheless, He has chosen to work through us, although we are filled with many limitations, to become His ambassadors. This confirms His identity as God and His divine plans for us proving that Love Reveals the Heart of God. It is on the basis of this revelation that the vision of *Love Reveals the Heart of God* was conceived and expressed in this book.

As Christian leaders, we must also focus on courtship, engagement, marriage, social living, Christian education, leadership counseling and parenthood within the church. Our aim must be to redefine the cultural aspects of Christianity as against religiosity. Christian leaders must ensure that misguided and misunderstood simulations do not override the holiness of what the Christian faith endorses. This book offers a spiritually and biblically based application that will help us to navigate our true assignment on earth. Remember that it is through the Love of God that His revelation is revealed.

This book contains many examples of relevant biblical references as well as several combined meditations on Love with a deeper application about God's mind and heart toward us. We see this in the account of Adam and Eve when the Lord asked the question: Where are you? God still sought out Adam and Eve even after their disobedience; this must be seen as the evidence of God's divine Love towards humanity; it reveals His heart as a heart of Love.

The stories concerning the lost coin, the lost sheep, and the lost soul of mankind are stories that reflect the tender Love that Jesus has for us all. This is also revealed through the account of Zaccheus.

ABOUT THIS BOOK

This book teaches about *agape* Love, and gives us an inside look into the heart of God in contrast with the heart of man. Within each page of this book is a new insight on spiritual intimacy with God. The writer identifies life-changing principles that are edifying to the soul and fundamental for Christian growth. He reminds us that our 'First Love' represents our covenant with God in which we become the object of God's desire each day. He also teaches that our relationship with our spouse is our first responsibility to God.

This book provides its readers with the knowledge of the true meaning of the Love of God. It introduces the concept of true Love that is spiritually ordained, physically based, and emotionally composed. This book presents models from a wide range of applications that are aimed to bring resolution in the family and the church, as well as helping us transcend thoughts and frozen feelings. **It provides a reference guide for counselors and others to study.** This book is suitable for home devotionals, workshops, seminars, and Bible studies and Sunday school lessons. There is no limitation on experiencing or knowing the true Love of God written in this book.

A copy of this book is available on www.meritshenry.org and in bookstores. Parts of this book and exercises can be freely downloaded from the website.

READING GUIDE

This book is about knowing and manifesting the Love of God. It is also a reference guide for learning how to model the Love of God; it teaches family values, church values, and social and relationship values, using stories from the Bible as well as from everyday experiences. It also serves as an application guide on how to assess Love at an individual and personal level.

This book can be read for the following purposes:

- Quick introduction to church converts: an object-oriented approach to Christ.
- Basic introduction and guide to Christian Education Department: an application model to Christ, an oriented approach for building a caring community, socialization, fellowship and sharing Christ.
- Full Teaching Model/Devotional Assessment used as an examination approach for all settings, serving as a tool to observe or identify dysfunctional behaviors.
- To promote basic unity within society and the church family. This book teaches about secularism, racism, cultural beliefs and religious beliefs.

— Merits Henry

Love

*L*ove is wonderful, Love is splendid and Love is magnificent! Love touches more people's life than any other actions: "*For God so loved the world that He gave His only Son...*" (John 3: 16, ESV). Love does not hurt; instead it brings life, joy, peace, comfort and forgiveness to humanity. Love has many wishes but one specific goal: please help me to Love always or even more.

Some major problems in today's society are as a result of a Love deficit. Love has many dimensions to it: it is like a breath of fresh air; it refreshes people's desires and feelings and it allows us to show appreciation and to be passionate and tender-hearted to one another. Nevertheless, our children can barely experience the fullness of God's Love through us because we ourselves do not truly understand the Love of God.

Love is difficult to describe. It is one of the most powerful forces that human beings can ever encounter. It has the ability to transform lives, and it gives healing from any kind of diseases. Alexie was diagnosed with cancer. Amazingly, the genuine Love of her family and friends caused them to seek the Lord on her behalf through fasting and prayer. As a result of their intercession, she experienced the supernatural healing of Christ. They testified that Love was the foundation of their intercession on her behalf before God (see James 5). "And so, we realize that Alexie's healing depended totally on genuine Love and prayer with the expression of God's Love."

Who cannot honestly conclude that Love is a treatment that eliminates the cancer of hurt, of bitterness and of unforgiveness?

Love is phenomenal! Love travels many miles to find peace and pursue it. Wherever the subject of her heart lies, she will go. Love heads home first to receive or to be graced with encouragement, appreciation and celebration. Love remembers all that she has. Love protects and cherishes. May you not only see but experience the virtue of Christ's Love in these pages.

Introduction

Through divine love, the revelation of God's creation is embraced.

There is nothing more powerful than Love. Love is the divine motivation for creation. It is the driving force and desire for a perfect world. The source of its inspiration will produce a successful generation. Nevertheless, despite the fact that Love is the most civil form of governance worldwide, whether it is on the basis of social relations or the pursuit of Christ, it is undeniable that its true manifestation is not being embraced within today's society. If it was, then there would not be wars, hatred, variance, prejudice, jealousy, abuse, greed, corruption, neglect racism, and injustice. Instead the world would be like the Garden of Eden when it was initially created. Regardless of how much people have tried to recreate this world, the fulfillment of hope and desire for the temporary pleasures of life will continue to elude our soul if we do not have Love.

Having the desires to be free to pursue one's personal dreams and to maximize one's potential in an attempt to make new discoveries is in fact a result of Christ's Love. The motivation and inspiration of dreams that sustain the passion of humanity, producing highly developed cultures and ideas, social systems, and religious classes has been extracted from the heart of God. This revelation is centralized in humanity's search for knowledge, and even more knowledge. Many have even tried to redefine the knowledge of God. Therefore, in order to comprehend the true concept of Love, one must understand the message of God. God is the sender of Love, as illustrated on the cross through His Son Jesus Christ.

Jesus' death is a result of Love. Love is the dynamic truth and will always be the foundation on which God communicates His purpose. Unfortunately, if Love is absent then the concept of knowing God is wrong, and consequently, the understanding will also be inaccurate and incomplete. This is because divine revelation is the manifestation of Christ's Love.

When I say "Love Reveals the Heart of God," I am not referring to daily chores or Love that is based on feelings, but rather:

- The ability to have a personal revelation of God in fellowship and obedience to His perfect will;
- The ability to have a personal relationship with Christ;
- The ability to relatively know Him through His Word;
- The ability to desire God;
- The ability to develop a relationship with the Word of God;
- The ability to personally know Him for yourself.
- The ability to know Him through sharing in His power, resurrection and suffering;
- To have an encounter with His presence;
- To understand the meaning and concepts of the cross;
- To understand the intense Love that Christ demonstrated on the Cross;
- The ability to practice the presence of His Love to our neighbors.

Many times our lives are nothing but a daily routine of struggles in which we try to stay afloat in the seas of uncertainties. We wrestle with pressing thoughts of yesterday, today and tomorrow. Our desires, passions and commitments are to be prosperous. We strive to gain positions of influence in order to accumulate financial wealth. We seek the power that money promises us. Nevertheless, the pursuit of Love among our brothers and sisters is predominantly self-centered. The world's heart has been preoccupied with the desire for power and dominion. It is blinded to unity, Love and respect among humanity. The effects of this self-centeredness can be easily observed in the world's devastating economic crisis.

Our failure to achieve care and control over the environment and circumstances has left us with a deep desire for change. We yearn for a transformation. Our spirit longs for a world where peace and contentment fuels spiritual and social uplifting.

Throughout the different world religions, there are various doctrines that promise reward which control circumstances and even death itself. The true results of these teachings are of paramount importance to the soul. Unfortunately, millions of people are deceived by these false doctrines. This is because Jesus is the only true source that is able to control all circumstances and death. After all, He is the only man to defeat death. It is quite interesting when we think of people's commitment, faith and belief to these false teachings. But while it may seem people follow different schools of thought, these people are really seeking to discover something greater than themselves: Love. The principal objective of our affection still has the same principle and motivation today as at the time of creation in Genesis. We want rediscover and retrieve that which we have lost: a rich fountain of Love, a perfect relationship with God, and of course our greatest desire which is to be in the Kingdom of God.

Ever since Adam's disobedience in the Garden of Eden, man's spiritual disconnection from his creator and his kingdom has taken on a new meaning. Instead of complete joy and comfort, man was presented with an official job description. Adam's disobedience should have resulted in death, but God instead showed him mercy and Love. Even though work was not a part of His initial plan, it was the preliminary provision for sin. From here on, man's relationship with God started to change because of man's choice to disobey. This system is still in existence today. On the other hand, the devil uses this as a means to distract us. His aspiration is to preoccupy us with work so that we are distracted from getting closer to God.

Is there a solution to the human dilemma? Yes!

- A Love relationship with God that will bring every answer, and meet every need in his life.
- A Father's heart: Love will motivate him to return home.
- A prodigal's heart to acknowledge the Love of Jesus by seeking first His Kingdom and righteousness.

One of the most resounding illustrations of God's Love occurs when Jesus declares His intention for man, "*I am come that they may have life and have it abundantly*" (John 10:10b, ESV). In this Scripture is the greatest declaration of redemption; hope and Love for mankind. It is the first official presentation of His message to mankind over two thousand years ago. Jesus unveiled and announced the problem and solution to mankind's dilemma in these simple words. He identifies the truth of His relationship with mankind, which means that mankind has a natural desire and inherent need to be restored by His Love.

It was never the intended purpose of God to demonstrate His Love this way toward us. Nevertheless, because of man's choice to seek otherwise, God had to make an alternate provision to save us. Until we are enlightened and set free by Jesus' Love, we will all be prisoners in the kingdom of darkness. All of us are born in a prison of sin. This is because of our sinful nature inherited from Adam. And so, this is the reason Jesus came to restore our relationship back with His Father, so that we can once again enjoy His promised peace, joy and Love.

To comprehend the desire of God's heart, it is necessary to understand His Love as well as His original purpose and intent for us. God created us for a specific reason. It is this inherited nature of Love that motivated God to create us—his spirit children, to share His Kingdom. Therefore, when we renounce the sinful nature which we received from Adam, and begin to walk in God's intended purpose we will start to inherit that which God created for us.

> *Are you tired? Worn out? Burned out on religion? Come to me. Get away with me and you'll recover your life. I'll show you how to take a real rest. Walk with me and work with me—watch how I do it. Learn the unforced rhythms of grace. I won't lay anything heavy or ill-fitting on you. Keep company with me and you'll learn to live freely and lightly.*
>
> —Matthew 11: 28–30, MSG

Love is God's divine plan for us. This is God's divine order for us. Discovering this divine truth is the divine secret of God's heart, as you read this book. Be ever blessed with divine Love, light and the life that is the true gift of God.

PART ONE

A Glimpse Into The Nature Of God's Heart

You will not only see but you will also experience.

"*We are not Christians unless the supreme motive of our lives be the Love of the Lord Jesus Christ*"

—Matt Jury, *The Prize of the Up-calling*

Therefore *shall a man leave his father and his mother,*
and shall cleave unto his wife;
and they shall become one flesh.

—Genesis 2:22–24,KJV

CHAPTER ONE

Understanding God's Design For The Family

The central reason God created the family unit was to glorify Himself and to advance His kingdom on earth. Nevertheless, many people view the family as a product of human invention to be used only for their convenience, their personal indulgence and their selfish desires. However, God's purpose for the family was to establish His kingdom on earth so that the generations that followed might come to acknowledge and glorify Him. Whether family is recognized by humanity as a divinely appointed institution or merely as a human invention, the word of the Lord affirms the importance of the family.

When God created the family unit, He intended for it to be the reflection of His own image on earth. It is through this institution, the covenant of a lifelong marriage between a man and a woman, as ordained by the Lord, that the generations to follow should be governed. Adam stated, as he referred to his wife: *"...this is bone of my bones and flesh of my flesh and she shall be called woman..."* (Genesis 2: 22–24, NIV). (See Isaiah 49:11 for further reference.) Lawmakers and justices of this world have used their logical reasoning to redefine God's definition of marriage and the family. Nevertheless, the word of God stands true and will never change. The Scriptures teaches that God will honor His Word above His name (Psalm 138:2). The name of Jesus is the most powerful force above any other name, yet His Word stands supreme and is greater by far.

The institution of the family was designed, by God to emphasize His First Love for mankind, through which the family would wisely accomplish the Lord's purpose, as commissioned by Him, to fulfill its responsibility. Man's covenant is unto the Lord, first, then to his family. There, the leader of the family must place his focus on Love and humility for his family, ensuring that his main goal be to personally walk with the Lord, and in doing so, revealing to the generation which is to follow the purpose of mankind's existence. Hence, the leader's duty is to identify the needs of his family by protecting them, providing for them, guiding them with Love, compassion and humility.

The Bible presents normative guidelines with strict commandments from the Lord, which must be followed as guides, to govern the life of the family, thus providing for much better moral and normal family relationship. Genesis 33:5; Psalm 78:1-8, Deuteronomy 4:9; 6:1-9; Proverbs 17:6; and Ephesians 6:1-4 are Scriptures that teach that the family is divinely mandated with specific tasks given to generate and maintain healthy relationships, which will explicitly nurture the Love of the Lord to meet the needs of mankind as the Holy Spirit guides. For this reason, in the pursuit of God's love, unfaithful practices between a man and his wife cannot be spiritually endorsed.

Disunity and independent goals at the expense of God's priceless matrimonial law cannot supersede His precious gifts, when He instructed that the man and the woman should fulfill their roles on earth. It was a command that 'they should multiply and replenish the earth.'

The replenishing of the earth is God's decreed covenant concerning the establishment of His earthly family. This covenant concerning the family is an endorsement by the Heavenly Father, which is also endorsed, in the New Testament by the Lord Jesus. Therefore, as the new covenant declares, a man should be the husband of only one wife with whom he takes the oath of marriage. (See 1 Timothy 3:2 and Titus 1:6.) This is God's exclusive design for the establishment of the family unit: to maintain a deeper Love, a newer commitment, a greater desire and a truer heart of leadership so that the generations to follow will see and come to glorify the Lord as their Heavenly Father.

Nothing can be more powerful than an intimate and obedient relationship with the Lord, which will fulfill and satisfy the longing of man's heart, thus assisting him in overcoming the lustful temptation of the flesh. Men are the shepherds of their home. Therefore, as fathers, it is man's duty to become positive role models for their children by displaying Christ-like leadership in the form of Loving, protecting, serving their family and by integrating devotional exercises of a spiritual nature so that they can effectively raise their children in the fear of the Lord. Their children will then learn to embrace a lifestyle of positive values and attitudes, beginning in the home, and then into the wider community, and into the generations which are to follow. Fathers are therefore the priestly stewards who have been given the divine responsibilities from the Lord to fulfill God's mandate, as good stewards on earth. Therefore, leaders of the family do not have the option of delegating or setting aside their parental obligations.

From A Biblical Love Perspective

The family that relies on God's sovereign covenant is one that clearly understands and demonstrates the effective functioning of God's concepts. This biblical prospective is foundational. As the Word of God declares,

> *...no one can serve two masters; for either he will hate the one and love the other, or he will be devoted to one and despise the other. You cannot serve God and money.*
> —Matthew 6:24, ESV

One should not be anxious for the necessities of life, nor can a person be committed to the things of this world and to the Kingdom of God, (Matthew 6:24–33), unless he has faith in the basis of his presupposition, which would embrace his revelation of God. Therefore, the approach taken should be on the basis of knowledge obtained from guidance under the authority of the holy Scriptures.

God has been in existence before the creation of humanity. In Him the nature of Love and holiness was formulated. His character of Love and holiness is the ultimate pattern for relationships. When God established the family by first creating Adam and Eve individually, He instituted the relationship of marriage. This institution is a lifelong covenant of commitment. This commitment is for the husband and the wife, as well as to glorify God whom both the man and woman must serve together (Genesis 2:21–24). This also confirms that the family relationship is divinely ordained, created and recognized by God as a holy institution.

Throughout the Scripture, the family is viewed as the first human institution ordained and designed to reflect God's image, and His Love on earth. This is established in an environment in which the family must fulfill God's commandments to further propagate the human race (Luke 10:27). Following God's design for the family, holy relationships will lead to a deeper understanding of God's Love for the family unit. With God's plan for the family, unity and togetherness will be achieved and will transcend individual differences.

> *"Many waters cannot quench love; rivers cannot sweep it away. If one were to give all the wealth of one's house for love, it would be utterly scorned..."*
> —Songs of Solomon 8:7, NIV

> *"She opens her arms to the poor and extends her hands to the needy"*
> —Proverbs 31: 20, NIV

> *"Now we who are strong ought to bear the weaknesses of those without strength of the weak and not just please ourselves"*
> —Romans 15: 1, NIV

Many problems that affect family relationships are the results of selfish attitudes. These selfish attitudes can be identified as the underlying problems that disrupt the flow of Love and unity in the family. God's grand design is also the overriding principle that affirms the power of Love through the Holy Spirit. This way, Love may be expressed in words and deeds, regardless of individuals' behavior, attitudes, or circumstances. This kind of Love is manifested when the needs of the family are first ministered to before the needs of self. (See John 15:12, Colossians 3:14 and John 14:12–17.) This kind of Love must always be exhibited to our family. It is the Holy Spirit of God which teaches wisdom and Love, the qualities necessary for effective family relationships. (See Galatians 5:13–15; 22-23.)

A relationship with God enables us to manifest the same qualities that Jesus exhibited in His relationship with people when He was on earth (see John 15.) God loves the family. (See John 17:20–26.) When we do not display Christ's Love, we are simply denying the work of Christ. The Bible teaches that when God redeems the people and indwells their lives, certain characteristics are formed, such as love, peace, joy, goodness, gentleness, faithfulness and self-control. Likewise, certain traits will be eliminated, such as jealousy, hatred, envy, selfishness and bitterness. The presence of the godly qualities and the absence of the negative characteristics produce Loving and lasting relationships in the family.

It is the father's duty as head of the family to encourage and develop good relationships within the home, relationships that will yield positive rewards in the daily life of his family. A father's first commitment is to God. Nevertheless, his first ministry is his family, as is the exercise of pursuing a career. Throughout the scriptures, we are encouraged to be compassionate and to be concerned with the welfare of others. For example, the Prodigal Son left home and did not acknowledge the kindness of his father. However, upon his return, his father showed him compassion and received him back into the family (Luke 15). This is to further imply that if compassion is implemented in our daily lives, it will clearly echo the teachings of Christ.

Many family disputes that end negatively are the result of a lack of compassion. How can we expect to exhibit a higher commitment to God whom we cannot see when we do not show Love to the people around us? We have to be willing to identify, acknowledge and confront the unpleasant root cause of our problems. When immediate problems like these are identified by the family, positive goals will be better incorporated to resolve each issue. Nevertheless, a gracious attitude with a devoted prayer life will lead to positive rewards.

USING THE BIBLE

All actions performed by God are formulated through His Love for mankind. Today we have the Scripture which records and demonstrates God's Love in action. The Love of God is the ever recurring theme in the Bible. Among all other books, the Bible is the only book that reveals to us God's purpose for our lives, through Christ who conquered death and hell for our redemption.

The Scripture teaches that Jesus Christ is the only hope of salvation, as His Spirit will always be with us remediating the soul in the midst of emotional problems and impure thoughts. The Bible is unlike any other books that are filled with affirmations and inspirational thoughts—those other books have been written from the background of accolades which one day will lose their authenticity. In-depth introspection and long periods of trying to evaluate the inerrancy of the Scriptures will always be counterproductive. But unless there are clear signals that our convictions are in line with biblical motivation, our leadership will be defiled and our respect will be eroded.

In the book of Revelation, a reproof was laid at the feet of the Church at Ephesus, which interestingly was known for its years of accomplishments. In fact, after reading through their long list of community services, one would certainly want to vote for them as 'The Church of the Year.' Christ said through the writings of John:

> *I know your works, your labor, your patience, and that you cannot bear those who are evil. And you have tested those who say they are apostles and are not, and have found them liars; and you have persevered and have patience, and have labored for My name's sake and have not become weary.*
>
> —Revelation 2:2–3, NKJV

Interestingly, after God had given those impressive lists of commendations, there was also a warning that if their deeds were not being done for the right reasons, the lampstand would be removed from their dwelling. That warning instigated by God was to inspire them to change and to remediate their impure motives. The motivational problem mentioned in the church at Ephesus was that they had left their First Love, which was their Love for Christ. How could that be? First, our Love for Christ must be our covenant of promise when our hearts experience the greatest joy of all, just like the streaming waters gushing forth from the 'head of a flowing river.'

The saints of Ephesus were rebuked for leaving their First Love. Again one may ask, how could first loving God be considered a broken relationship with others? God's words are filled with Himself and not with vain promises; he demonstrates His own nature. However, we should observe that the word 'first' here is not a matter of first in time or first in everything, but denotes a matter of first in priority and in responsibility. In other words, the Ephesians were no longer doing their first work of ministry preference and family protocol with Love and a sense of gratitude because they loved the Lord, but rather for lesser reasons that were required by the Lord. The lesser reasons may have been for affirmation of others, for the praise of men, or perhaps they had acted out of duty or guilt. It is often hard to understand why at times, we do the opposite of what God has called us to do. Is it because we are not willing to adhere to the truth of His Word?

It is not difficult to do the things that God has called us to do, as we need to apply the Word of God to our lives for the sake of our family, and for demonstrating our Love for the Lord to the world. This attitude will display a sense of loyalty to God and to our family, knowing that our Lord and Savior to whom we owe all things is first in our lives.

The way in which we present our family and our ministry to the Lord, is a reflection of our Love for Him. In like manner, with an attitude of Love, God expects us to care for others in ways that are fully expressive of our appreciation for their friendship and as an expression of God's Love within us. A heart that is searching for ways to express Love will strive for and will be ready to face any adversity that comes because it is not responsive to or dependent on external solutions. Instead, it is solely an undaunted flow of grateful expression from that will capture the respect and value of others. Expressing gratitude through Love instead of grumbling is a worthy statement of Love to our Lord and to our family. Ministering to others is doing something—everything—for the one we Love the most,
It is essential that all Christians manifest and share their Love with those around them. This will allow us to exercise direct responsibility and moral understanding in following God's design. By doing so, we will all be fulfilling the mandate of our Lord.

THE HUSBAND'S ROLE: SUBMIT IN LOVE AND SUPPORT

The Bible affirms that the husband should exercise His leadership position in the spirit of Love and as a servant, using Jesus' ministry as an example. This means the husband's major role is to serve his family (see Colossians 3: 16–19, 21, Ephesians 6:4) with Love, and not with a controlling attitude over them. The husband should be willing to sacrifice himself for the protection of his family, praying for them always, as he provides for the physical and spiritual needs of his wife and his children. With such high standards expected of him, his first duty is not to put his own personal desires ahead of his family (Joshua 24:15). This direct command is the order of God's design (1 Timothy 5:7–8; Genesis 3:17–18) and teaches us that it is the man's responsibility to care for and to provide financial support for his wife and for his children. It is not the will of God that the man should expect his wife to work outside of the home for merely the purpose of a higher standard of living (1 Timothy 6:8).

The example of Love, which God has given to the husband to guide him, is essential for his daily walk with the Lord. It is also an act of deeper sacrifice, obedience and unconditional commitment for as Christ Loves the Church, so are husbands to Love their wives (Ephesians 5). Christ is the progenitor of Love, therefore, He expects us to Love our wives as He Loves the church. To Love the way that the Lord Loves is a measure of our character as it also shows excellence. This example also teaches that such an expression of Love exemplifies Christ's Love for the church. On the subject of Love, it is the duty of the husband to Love his wife, as Christ Loves the church. This Love is a called 'duty expression' because it glorifies God to the world.

When a husband or a wife follows the example of Jesus' by saying, "I Love you," it becomes an essential ingredient for a happy marriage. We can then accommodate our spouse unconditionally through a life of 'for better or worse, in sickness and in health, till death do us part.' That is the way of true Love when it is poured out of a sincere heart of unconditional Love as ordained by the Lord. In his book *A Successful Marriage,* Dr. Christopher states that: "Love is that strong cord that ties two hearts together in marriage. Thus without Love, no one can enjoy a successful relationship."[1]

According to Solomon:

> *...Love is strong as death...Many waters cannot quench love, neither can the floods drown it: if a man would give all the substance of his house for love, it would utterly be condemned.*
> —Song of Solomon 8:6, 7, KJV

Love secures our future for our eternal destiny in Christ. It is the most essential element of a happy and fulfilled marriage. Nothing can take the place of sincere Love in a marriage. No beauty, fame, luxurious cars or expensive homes can be substituted for genuine Love. Love is matchless. *"Love never fails"* (1 Corinthians 13:8, NIV).

---

1 Christian Marriage and Family, 1987 – 2002, G. A. Christopher, ed., International Ministerial Bible College, President, Agege, Logos, Nigeria, Vol. 2.

The absence of Love, the lack of appreciation and the absence of understanding are qualities that are born within the heart of the man who is having problems in spending time with God and in His Word. He becomes the object of great compromise in his responsibilities, and this is not beneficial for a successful family life.

How can we reflect an image of integrity in the eyes of God if we intentionally continue to struggle with the deeds of the flesh? The whole idea of Love was never a struggle in God's heart. This should be our concern. Lack of genuine Love diminishes our reverence for God and, over time, it manifests and builds troubles in the heart. This enables the mind to focus on unholy thoughts which lead to unrighteousness. (See Ecclesiastes 3:16–22.)

The enemy is a deceptive opponent who lures us away from our vows and from our commitments to the Lord and to our family. The expression of our attitude and of our heart for staying faithful to our 'First Love' with our Lord, and also in our marriage is potentially affected. This is crucial to a successful family life. We should endeavor to terminate any covenant we had with Satan in order for us to be identified with our loving Lord.

The Scriptures assure us that if we confess our sins, God is faithful and just to forgive all our shortcomings. (See 1 John 1:7.) Anyone who covers his sins will never prosper, but whoever confesses and renounces his or her sins will be protected by God's Love. Give this relationship to the Lord Jesus. We will be reassured, encouraged and uplifted as He strengthens and transforms our lives into a position of greater and deeper understanding of Love and into a more wonderful adventure of life filled with the divine Love of Almighty God.

Dr. Christopher has made an interesting comment, by stating that:

Love is much more than a physical, intimate relationship. It is the desire to share, to cherish, and if needs be, to sacrifice for each other; such Love makes the adjustment of marriage much easier to accomplish. [2]

As the Word of God reveals, a man should carefully analyze his motives or his aim when desiring to choose a wife. If he desires to impart genuine Love, his objective should not be the overshadowing of his spiritual,

2 Ibid.

social and physical responsibilities for his new family. Instead, he has to take on the responsibility to intercede with the Lord on behalf of his family and to seek the blessing of God through regular prayer and devotion for them (1 Timothy 2: 8; 1 Peter 3: 7; and Numbers 6: 7–11). The frequency with which a man prays for his family will determine his appreciation for his household. Husbands are commanded to Love their partners even as Christ Loves the church.

Marrying a woman within the parameters of 'First Love' unto God is God's design. This is because our 'First Love' must represent our covenant to the Lord, for this is God's perfect will. Having a wife is a reflection of the Church as the bride of Christ. Therefore, one of God's instructions related to marriage is not to marry the woman with whom we think we are in Love with—as Samson, Solomon, Ahab and David did—but to Love the woman we marry, as Boaz did when he married Ruth. Although Boaz was a man of wealth and power, he was humble enough to respect and assist in the conversion of the Gentile woman, Ruth. Above all, he was wise in his admiration of her courage, devotion, kindness, and faithfulness to Naomi, her mother-in-law (Ruth 2:11).

The task laid upon husbands is greater than that of the wives because as husbands we are told to model our Love after Christ, His Church and His death. The pattern given is in reference to Christ's sacrificial Love as He laid down His life for us all. As husbands we are to do the same for our wives by paying the utmost price in unbroken commitments and sacrifices for them even when we are deeply wounded. In such cases, we are to Love our wives and go the extra mile to resolve, relinquish and rebuild the wall of Love if it has been broken. Jesus did it for us, and in essence, we are to do the same for our wives by making daily and genuine sacrifices for them as we mortify the desires of our own uncommitted, selfish ways and self-centered ambition. Thus, this must be done if we are to model Christ's design and meet our wives' deepest expectations. Stephen and Alex Kendrick state: "The example that God gives to the husband to follow is simply the most courageous and sacrificial act ever done in all the history of humanity."[3]

Boaz enacted Christ-like Love and the five essential components of a leader when he noticed Ruth. Ultimately, he considered himself blessed

---

3 Ibid, Resolution for Men

to be wanted by a woman whom he believed could have gone after a more youthful companion (Ruth 3:10). Boaz's kindness and admiration was so overwhelming that Ruth asked him: *"Why have I found such favor in your eyes that you notice me—a foreigner?"* (Ruth 2:10, NIV) The Scripture declares that Boaz noticed her. In Hebrew the word "notice" means to "acknowledge with honor, and desire to understand." This is what Love does. Boaz did not simply see her; he understood and revered her as a call to preserve the family's honor.

The prophet Isaiah declares:

> *But yet in it shall be a tenth, and it shall return, and shall be eaten: as a teil tree, and as an oak, whose substance is in them, when they cast their leaves: so the holy seed shall be the substance thereof.*
> —Isaiah 6:13, KJV

God's promise is that a small remnant of people would believe and be preserved by Isaiah's word of knowledge. Likewise, God demonstrated His covenant and promise of salvation through Ruth and Boaz.

Boaz proved himself to be a provider, a protector, an intercessor, a cover, and a redeemer for the generations that followed after him. As we Love others, God will reveal the character of His Love in us, so that we can express our Love as experienced from His heart to our partners. Boaz understood that Ruth was more than the culmination of her past misfortunes and present circumstances. Boaz thought that he could honor the honest person that Ruth was and the person that she could become if he became her cover for a better life.[4]

God desires for us to see Ruth and Boaz's union as an example of how He sees us, how much He Loves us, and how He has redeemed us for Himself, especially those of us who would feel as though the cares of life have ravaged our potential, purpose and hopes for redemption.

---

4 Aisha Long – Bascom, "Recognizing Your Boaz: Getting a Second Chance" ,http://simplylola.blogspot.ca

The Wife's Role: Submit In Love With Obedience

The Scripture uses the analogy of Christ as a reference to illustrate the duty and function of the wife to her husband (Ephesians 5:22-24, Colossians 3:18.) This illustration reveals the relationship of Christ and His bride, which is a prototype of Love and obedience. The wife is summoned by the Word of God to willingly submit to the ordinance of her husband in Love and obedience as unto God. It is worth noting that the Scripture does not support the wife's submission to anything demanded by her husband that is contrary to the will of God. Additionally, the Scriptures teach that the wife has the authority to respectfully rebuke her husband as his sister in the Lord if his acts are contrary to the teachings of Christ (2 Peter 3:6). Nevertheless, if such measures are needed, it should be done with the spirit of gentleness, without intimidation and without negative criticism (Galatians 3:5 and 2 Peter 3:1-5).

According to the Scripture, the wife's primary role is to nurture her children in the admonition and fear of the Lord. This also includes managing the home with the aim of creating an environment that is conducive to spiritual growth. The environment should be Christ centered (1 Timothy 5:10, 14; Titus 2: 4-5; Proverbs 31:10-31). On the other hand, the wife should also recognize her role as fulfilling the call of God and not as a capitulation as portrayed in some cultures that teach that work has no value unless it comes with monetary rewards.

Understanding God's design for the wife is important as she has no need to seek her own identity as her identity is intertwined with that of her husband. A wife's desire should only be for her husband, her standard bearer, whose duty it is to Love her. They must endeavor to build a relationship of communication and of Love as the husband patiently and openly honors and supports her. This is by way of providing a place of security that is conducive to godly living as he daily lay down his life for her.

When we follow God's design and understand His will for our lives, glorious things will happen through us as husbands. Husbands thus become God's priests, flowing with unchanging thoughts of greater Love for their family as Christ shed His blood for His church. Hence, as God's family, we become vessels that the Lord can fill with His unconditional Love for the next generation. (See Psalm 24:6.) When we access salvation through God's Love, He will reveal the never-ending source of His Love to us. This is the key to understanding His thoughts toward us as we will never be able to access salvation on our own initiative. With such affirmation, it clearly denotes that we are saved by the power of God's Love with His grace, and not by the works of men. It was never based on us alone. God Loved Adam and from Adam He created Eve, and returned her to Adam, and they became one flesh. Therefore, God's Love begins with relationship. The Scripture states that: "*Can two walk together except they be agreed?*" (Amos 3:3, KJV)

FAMILY RELATIONSHIP

Family relationship is the most powerful bond designed by God. There is no other institution that can be compared to the heart of God as much as the family. It is constituted by God's design and physically comprised of individuals related by marriage, bloodline, or adoption

The family serves as an essential part of God's kingdom on earth. Adam and Eve were the first family created by God. They became the origin of all other families on earth. Adam, the priest of the family, was responsible for the decisions made within the family. Whenever his decisions were wisely made, his family prospered. Whenever he chose to disobey God's rule, his family was negatively impacted. Adam's sinful nature of disobeying God was also imputed to his children. When Cain killed his brother Abel, God could no longer work through and communicate with him. Nevertheless, on the basis of the covenant of Love, God made provisions for the restoration of the family. God provided Seth as a means of establishing a new family on earth (Genesis 4: 25). Through this process, God's program of establishing new families continued through the lineage of Noah, Abraham and Jacob in order that His plans might be fulfilled on earth through the family.

The next significant person after Adam and Eve was Noah, a virtuous man who believed and followed the righteous principles of God. He and his family survived the greatest flood of all because of their obedience to the Lord (Genesis 6). They were physically protected and spiritually guided in the ark as God had designed it, a typology of God's salvation and Love for mankind. God's perfect design was preserved again for Noah and his family as He had done for Adam and Eve by bringing forth Seth.

Today, God is searching for righteous men who will again represent the ark of salvation by completely obeying His will as Noah did, righteous men who will first manifest the Love of God to their family, and will effectively minister their duties as provider, prophet, priest and king of their home. It should be the joy of all men's hearts when they see their family first as their ministry, and will then provide for them a home of security and protection from the evils of this world. Their first ministry should be to do everything for the ones they Love the most.[5] They should confidently believe that this is God's design for their family. Noah played a glorious evangelical role in his family. He ministered the Word of God unto his household. He introduced his family to the Lord by his obedience to the Word of God. Noah knew God's design, and he followed God's blueprint for his life and for the lives of his family. As evidence, he and his family were completely saved. God will never destroy the family that is being obedient to His will and command; instead, He will provide the means of escape and restoration, and the means for their salvation even in the midst of disaster. (See Lot's wife as reference in Genesis 19:26.)

God is entreating the leader of the family to first make the change that will bring eternal life to him and to his household, to gain access to salvation, and to be free from sin and from the cares of this life. An individual may consider his life is a failure in terms of personal achievement because of a lack of faith in the Lord in the choice of career or even in the choice of a marriage partner, but one must realize that God is a re-designer of life and He is also the master for ensuring successes out of failures. He has done it many times before and He is able, willing and just to do it again.

God can transform broken relationships, turning them into the most loving, admirable, successful and dynamic relationships, as one's faith allows him to do. Furthermore, God will accelerate the results that one has been longing for; He will motivate one's desire to Love and to value one's earnest desires again. God will also maximize the strength and courage that one need to forgive the most unpleasant situation. He can also make provisions for new and better things.

After a while, Noah became a drunkard by gratifying the desires of his flesh through the lascivious motives of Satan. Eventually his sons went their own ways and forgot about God. Their descendants fell into idol

---

5 Ibid, 232

worship and other forbidden practices. However, when it would appear that God could no longer accomplish his purpose through people after another violation of man's responsibility to him, ten generations after Noah's fall, God spoke with Abram, a descendant of the son of Shem.

Through a heart of Love, God's intended purpose unfolded again in Genesis 12. He chose Abram by calling him out from among his family of idol worshippers. God's plan was to establish His righteousness through another generation by redeeming them from idol worship. This was also done to preserve the lineage of the coming Messiah, Jesus Christ. As he obeyed the voice of God, and left his family's cultic practices, God changed his name from Abram to Abraham. In doing so, God revealed Himself to Abraham and made a new covenant with him, declaring that, he, the Lord, would make of him a great nation.

Beginning with Abraham to his son Isaac, continuing through his sons Esau and Jacob, God was working towards His model–the family. He appeared to Jacob as He had appeared to Abraham and spoke the same words, "I will make you a great nation" (Genesis 12:2, NKJV). God cannot operate in failure, meaning that He specifically designed the family to succeed and to live in the abundance of life, as He again established a new covenant with mankind. Through the lineage of Abraham to Israel, God created a new family, which today is inherently blessed and prosperous with the blessings declared in Deuteronomy 28 and in Numbers 6. From Abraham's generation to Israel's generation and into the New Testament period, God's design for the family never changed. Regardless of the many inappropriate models that emerged, after promising starts, those were always rejected by the Lord.

Through Moses, God delivered the Israelites from bondage, brought them in to the desert and again made a covenant with them, telling them essentially, "You will be my people and I will be your God. I will lead you into the land I promised your forefathers."[6] In other words, God promised to be their father and that they would be his family.

The Scriptures show that God loves the family. One of His designs is to be our king by making us citizens of His Kingdom. Joshua caught this revelation when he declared his loyalty to the Lord with his family.

---

6 Myles Munroe, "Rediscovering the Kingdom" (Shippensburg, PA: Destiny Image Publishers, Inc., 2004), 33 – 63.

He stated: "*As for me and my house we will serve the Lord*" (Joshua 24:15b, NASB).

Another design of God's purpose for the family is that the family must be of service to Him. We were created to serve the Lord with our gifts. Paul also was inspired when he wrote on God's design for the family. He wrote to Ephesian Church, "*For we are God's masterpiece. He has created us anew in Christ Jesus, so we can do the good things he planned for us long ago*" (Ephesians 2:10, NLT).

In the five chapters of Ephesians, Paul again outlines God's design for the family in a step-by-step manner:

· Walk in Love
· Walk in light
· Walk in wisdom
· Value the worth of a good relationship

Abraham was not perfect, yet the Lord was able to use him to bring greater blessings to the world through his family. God uses the family as His platform to expand His Kingdom, holiness, and good purposes on earth. He uses this operative principle to teach the world about His Love through the family so that His Love can become contagious in affecting the world.

Throughout history, God was setting the stage and preparing an environment for His Son's appearance. It was through one of these families that God brought Jesus into the world (Matthew 1 and 2). Out of this order, God created a new family and called this family, this called-out remnant, this *ecclesia*, His Church. As a result, it is possible today for us to be a part of a body of people where we all can encounter the presence of God as a family. God the Father sacrificed His own Son so that we could be adopted into His family as His children. This blessed hope is what keeps our faith unmovable and steadfast and what thus encourages us not to grow weary in well-doing.

The family represents the church, in that, without the strong family, the church and the society would be weakened. Out of this came the godly family which is being directed by the Holy Spirit. With God's Love in our hearts, the fruit of producing godly children and having a successful home will always be seen from generation to generation. It is said that, when the family is strong then Christ can develop His wonderful plans for the church. God's design is depicted in the family and the church. The family is a reflection of the church. In like manner, the church is also a figure of the family. So, in essence, a healthy family builds a strong church, and a spiritual church maintains godly families. In other words, God designed the family as the Church to be successful.

The Scripture declares that we are the Bride of Christ. We are also the family of God; according to John 8:31–36, God views us as His family, and not as households of servants. Therefore we are all joint heirs with Christ Jesus (Romans 8:12). Similarly, God expects us to value our family. He expects that, as we demonstrate our godly assigned duties to our family (Ephesians 5:22–32), we will also serve Him in faithfulness.

God created the family so that the family will demonstrate to the generation to follow the blessedness of being the sons of God. From the beginning, God wanted His children to relate to Him in Love, as children, and not as slaves or hired servants who would obey Him out of obligation. With the old covenant, servants would relate to their masters on a superficial level, as there was no intimacy or sense of family connection in such relationship; but under the new covenant, sons and daughters are transposed as heirs and joint heirs with Christ. As heirs, they will then inherit the parents' fortune. Paul uses this analogy as a reminder to teach us the lesson of Romans 8:15 which states: *"For ye have not received the spirit of bondage again to fear; but ye have received the spirit of adoption, whereby we cry Abba Father"* (Romans 8:15, KJV). The two most important truths we learn from God's Word about the family are that God is the creator of the family and also that God Loves His family. When He created Adam and Eve, He commanded them to be creative, to be fruitful, to multiply and to replenish the earth. God created us to be a loving family unit. He expects us as His creation to take delight in our experiences and in our relationships (Proverbs 5:18–19). Husbands and wives, according to God's design must be of one body and of one mind (1 Corinthians 7). So, then, therefore, we can safely say, the family was designed to:

1. Represent God in this world—from the husband, a divine and genuine Love for his bride should be the hallmark. From her heart, the wife must express compassion to her husband and as a mother, she should Love and care for her children as she becomes a figure of divine light to her family.

2. Replenish—to manifest his eternal purpose to represent God's Kingdom on earth, through his Love and wisdom. We find the first description of God's will for man in the charge to be fruitful, multiply and replenish the earth. This is a commandment of the Lord that the man should desire his wife with faithfulness and Love in their procreation of the next generation.

3. Prepare the Next Generation (Deuteronomy 6:4–9 and Psalm 78:1–8) as the training ground to receive the seed for future harvest. It is the duty of the family to train and nurture their children in the fear of the Lord. The church's responsibility is to act as the facilitator, preparing the mind of everyone concerning the things of the Lord.

4. Divinely show Love through the ministry of the family.

To demonstrate the importance of the heavenly family, Jesus, when told of His earthly family's desire to see Him, responded by stating: "*For whosoever shall do the will of my Father which is in heaven, the same is my brother, and sister, and mother...*" (Matt 12:50, KJV). It is important that we understand the illustration that Jesus was demonstrating to the scribes and Pharisees. Not that Jesus was dishonoring or disrespecting His earthly family, but He showed the people that His first mission was to the world. Jesus uses this principle also to bring forth the lesson of priority. In everything there is a first; as Jesus was busy ministering to the crowd, His immediate family was also there, but His main focus was to the lost family—the world. While it must have been very difficult for His family to understand, Jesus had to balance His mission as He traveled, preaching and reaching out to the lost while assuring His earthly family of His purpose.

A BALANCED RELATIONSHIP

Balance is an important family concept. It is like developing a business idea or vision that takes serious commitment. Many people today, including entrepreneurs and business owners, have learned the art of flexibility and the maximizing of business opportunities; and they have used it in balancing their schedule. It is said that over fifty-one percent of business owners have cited flexibility as their way of achieving a healthy balance in their business and personal lives. Nevertheless, only twenty–one percent have admitted to scheduling quality time with their family, while only eleven percent admitted to leaving their job to honor their family commitment.

From a worldly prospective, business benefits considerably from competitiveness and people desire financial security. Making a commitment to the family is significant. Even though balance is an excellent method used to maximize opportunities, passion and energy on business and family, its priority must be honored in accordance with God's design.

The family's commitments must be first, regardless of one's business schedule. In one of his epistles to the church on devotion to God and family, Paul asserted:

If anyone speaks, they should do so as one who speaks the very words of God. If anyone serves, they should do so with the strength God provides, so that in all things God may be praised through Jesus Christ. To him be the glory and the power forever and ever, Amen.
—1 Peter 4:11, NIV

The Apostle Paul concludes by highlighting some general rules, by which every man may regulate his conscience and practice, "…that whether they eat, or drink, or whatsoever they do, they should do it all with a habitual aim to the glory of God. It is worth considering his precepts, the propriety, the expediency, the appearance, and the tendency of their actions"[7] (Arthur W. Pink). Paul's teachings were directed to everyone as a reminder to honor their family's commitment as such honor brings glory to the Lord. God honors family on the principles seen in 1 Samuel 2:30:

Therefore, the Lord, the God of Israel declares: "I promised that members of your father's family would minister before me forever. But now the LORD declares: 'Far be it from me! Those who honor me I will honor, but those who despise me will be disdained…'
—I Samuel 2:30, NIV

---

7 Arthur W. Pink, "Divine Guidance," ttp://www.monergism.com

Troubled times are everywhere. This divinely inspired counsel comes to us very clearly. Doctors' offices are filled with individuals who are beset with emotional problems as well as physical impediments. Divorce courts are overflowing because of unresolved family problems. Human resource administrators and counselors work long hours in an effort to assist in helping to resolve family issues.

Family time has been deprived in many dimensions, much like the family life of the prodigal son who took his portion and left his father's home. This sort of behavior has driven many relationships into unknown territories because one had not sought the counsel of the Lord before embarking on one's journey (Proverb 19:20–21). Remember, the prodigal son, who embarked in pride, on his failed journey without consulting with the Lord? It is likely that he had not set long-term goals in the event he was unable to fulfill his short-term goals. His decision lacked insight and the blessing of his father; therefore he failed in his pursuit of a new life.

As required, it was the duty of the prodigal son to first set some positive goals; he had not consulted with his father and neither did he seek his father's advice before making his crucial decision. It is quite obvious that he never did, which showed the lack of trust and the blatant disregard he had for his father. Could there have been perhaps an enmeshment in the relationship between the son and his father? Yes, there might have been, but the earlier instigation on the son's part to leave his father's home without first seeking his blessing also revealed the young man's immaturity and his selfish motives.

His expectations were shattered after he had wasted his fortune on luxurious living. He became physically, spiritually and mentally affected as a result of his selfish mistakes, after which he became extremely remorseful. The words of an old proverb state: "Sometimes we must hit the bottom before we are able to rise to the top and regain our senses and recognize our faults." Like the prodigal son, many have walked away and have left their family wounded and devastated. But as members of one family, individuals must place special values on the time they spend with their family. If not, an environment will be created that will make it difficult for anyone to believe that a passionate and successful relationship with the family can be maintained. Time spent together, as a family must be conducive to the family structure in order to create a loving and harmonious relationship.

Nothing is wrong with asking for the blessings of the leader of the family unit. It is also God's desire that one should set lofty goals and work towards achieving them. (See Psalm 37:4.) It is within the context of the total man that God creates each person and allows him to make individual choices. However, there are many ways in which to approach the setting of one's goals. Some individuals may set their goals based on the needs of their family, while others set goals according to the financial needs of their family. Others take a wider view of their life and pursue their goals and dreams from a more modest perspective.

However, some individuals are quitters and therefore, they are more liable to failure. Nevertheless, it does not matter how one sets his goals; it is very important for one to consider the reason why God created the human race. As Christians, we should aim at nothing but the best; in the words of William Carey, we should, "Attempt great things for God and expect great things from God." We cannot afford to quit or remain lukewarm. Rather by faith, diligence and determination, we should press towards the goal and win. Therefore, for this reason we should always aim high for God and expect to be elevated, because we are born not to fail, but born to win. The fact that the younger brother, the prodigal son, instigated the early division of the family's estate showed his rebellious attitude and the dishonor that he had brought to his father, thus undermining his father's authority.

We were created as one family but each of us has independent thoughts. Like a cake which is made up of different ingredients, each person's idea is paramount in determining who that person really is. But also, each person must assess his own situation separately from that of others, when he assesses his own goals. A prominent American judge was asked what citizens of each country of the world could do to reduce crime and disobedience to law and order, and bring peace and contentment to the lives of each nation's citizens. He carefully responded, "I would suggest a return to the old-fashioned practice of prayer time and family serenity."[8] One could certainly agree with the comment made by this learned judge, Harry Anderson. Family time spent in prayer is the wisdom of a healthy relationship.

Achieving a balanced relationship takes a concentrated effort by all members within the family unit; if there is failure to impart proper care

---

8 Harry Anderson and Thomas S. Monson, "Come unto Him in Prayer and Faith" http://www.lds.org/2009.

and attention with godly Love and purpose, undue problems will arise. For example, because God created us as spiritual beings, our duty is to Love Him with our whole heart, soul, body, and spirit (Matthew 22:37–40). This further illustrates to us that our goals are to be in agreement and balance with our spiritual convictions.

If our goals appear to be against what the Lord has asked of us, then we will eventually become emotionally fragmented, spiritually bankrupt and intellectually deficient. Eventually, we will lose our joy and enthusiasm to be who the Lord meant for us to be. Moreover, because God created us as emotional human beings, the arm of connection through socialization and companionship must be ever present. However, if we neglect the social integration of our life and practice the 'all work and no play' model, then we will soon find ourselves out of balance with reality, and thus we will eventually begin to experience physical, emotional, social, and spiritual isolation. Spiritually and socially, the Lord expects us to become enlightened and socially balanced, and be aware of who we really are; as we learn to balance our relationship with our family and with the Lord, we aspire to satisfy the five dimensions of our being, as persons:

- Spiritual Being;
- Family Relationship;
- Social Integration with Others;
- Physical Makeup; and,
- Work and Real Life Aspirations.

We should always examine ourselves, first in light of what God has intended for our lives, before setting our goals and before embarking on our journey in terms of what we hope to achieve. We should consider the aspirations that we are aiming for; we should set our goals with the aim of achieving a holistic and well-rounded family unit and we must ensure that we do not fail in the context of the total person whom God has intended us to be.

In thankfulness, the prodigal son discovered his true identity and what he had walked away from, as he passionately returned to his father's house; but in the beginning, he had problems and subsequently, he lost his identity. In ignorance, the son failed to aspire to be the person whom his father had intended him to be. But when he came to the knowledge of what he had left behind, and what he had become, he repented and returned home to his father's bosom. In humbleness he declared: "*Father I have sinned against heaven and in thy sight, and am no more worthy to be called thy son*" (Luke 15:21, KJV). With open and loving arms, his father received him. This is an example of the heavenly Father's Love for His earthly children, even when they have failed Him.

There is therefore no doubt that God has a purpose for our lives. As His earthly family, He created us, His children, to be priests and kings, not servants, placing within us the gifts of eternal life. However, we must be mindful not to neglect the sealed covenant of this earthly relationship and the responsibility by which it is governed (Ephesians 1:13).

We must all remember God's plan for His children; He promised that He will teach us His ways and that He will lead and guide us through the path that He has prepared for us, so that we will achieve our true purpose both here on earth and in heaven. The Word of the Lord states: "*I will instruct thee and teach thee in the way thou shalt go: I will guide thee with mine eye*" (Psalm 32: 8, KJV). God's blessedness of forgiving His children is His sealed covenant with us.

Above all, it is important that we stay within the concept that the Lord has set forth as a model by which we must adhere. We must remember that it is the will of our Lord that we, as His earthly families, develop and maintain healthy and holistic relationships with one another as we strive to achieve our earthly goals, while we commit ourselves to His will. A successful relationship requires godly commitment as we maintain forgiveness towards one another, as He has forgiven us.

A balanced relationship is built on a number of godly principles: maintaining our communication with the Lord through His Word, and balancing our relationship with our family and with our community. These are the most important foundational principles on which successful relationships with the Lord and with the family are founded. It is also important that all members of the family be involved in the affairs of the Lord, as well as in the daily social and spiritual well-being of the community in which the family resides. This too is a foundational requirement, as ordained by the Lord, from the foundation of the world. "*...Love thy neighbor as thyself*" (Matthew 22:39, KJV).

Nevertheless, there are times when the demands of other daily commitments do interfere with the quality time that should be devoted to the family and most importantly, to the work of the Lord. However, the demands of the family and other social commitment can and will create a vacuum in the spiritual life of the one who leads, thus creating both physical and psychological dysfunctions within the family unit. Such conditions can and will expose the family to negative connotations in their Christian walk, which of course may eventually lead to attacks by the enemy. The leader of the family must ensure that he is prayerfully watching and communicating with the Lord in prayer.

Even a pious devotion or a faithful commitment to the community, to the Lord and to the family, if not managed wisely, though performed with the best of intention, can become a monumental concern that leads to misunderstanding. Therefore, every effort must be made by the leader of the family to be engaged in meaningful and mutual dialogue with the family and with the Lord while giving service to others. Thus, the thought of becoming engaged in compromising situations will not be entertained. Also great efforts ought to be made by the priest of the family to ensure that respect, Love and appreciation for one another are maintained; and that, should indeed, be the daily theme within the family unit. Such commitment will enhance a deeper Love, a more trusting and stable relationship and a greater understanding among members of the family, which at the end will fulfill the divine will of the Lord on earth.

Never forget that above all the Lord is the head of the family and His divine purpose must be done through spiritual leadership. He declares: *"Let your light so shine before men that they may see your good works and glorify your father who is in heaven"* (Matthew 5:16, KJV). Remember, it is through the ordained earthly family that the world will come to know and glorify the Lord.

The Lord is passionate concerning His relationship with His earthly family. He has uniquely fashioned us and imparted within us the desire to serve Him; the desire to express our gratitude to Him for His divine Love, guidance and protection, which He has bestowed on us. Above all, He has divinely and uniquely imparted within us the ability to understand the ways in which we ought to define our relationship with Him and with our family, so that the generations to follow will see Him through us and come to glorify Him also as their Lord and Savior.

The Lord demands that He be the main priority and the most important entity in our lives, which is the first of all commandments. He states: "*...thou shalt Love the Lord thy God with all thy heart, and with all thy soul and with all thy mind. This is the first and great commandment*" (Matthew 22:37–38, KJV). The second commandment, which is just as important states: "*... thou shalt love thy neighbor as thyself, there is none greater commandment than these*" (Mark 12:31, KJV).

The intended declaration of these words were to enlighten us when Jesus first mentioned the principles of giving service to Him, as He states: "*...Seek ye first the kingdom of God, and his righteousness; and all these things shall be added unto you*" (Matthew 6:33, KJV). God's ultimate goal is to teach us that the greatest of all our security and the most valuable investment of all are found when we understand the differences between our relationship with our Lord, with the family and with our community; after which, He will bless us with earthly rewards.

Our first priority, above all, is for us to: "*Love the Lord your God with all your heart and all your soul and all your mind and all your strength*" (Mark 12:30, NIV). This is the order in which we must prioritize our relationship: with the Lord, with the family and with others. The Lord must be first in all things. When God is at the center of our lives, everything else falls into place. After this, He will give us the grace, the endurance and the wisdom to demonstrate greater Love and devotion to our family. He will also give us the ability to impart to others the grace that He Himself has bestowed on us.

Love goes beyond normal duties when we allow the light of God to shine in our lives, and above all, Love remains when all else fails. Many times we have failed miserably, but God's mercies still embrace and uphold us through it all. His never-ending Love breaks all barriers; it goes beyond the complaints, it makes the way where there is no way, and through His Love, He reveals His heart to us. "His Love is greater far than pen or tongue, can ever tell." That is true Love! As the song writer states that he: "Rescues the perishing and he cares for the dying..." Therefore, we are to Love the Lord beyond measure, and serve our family with faithfulness as we continue to experience the Love of God as was radiated through His Son's shed blood at Calvary. Let the world see His Love shining in our heart so that they too can come and glorify the risen Christ.

Justice, truth and grace were revealed through the death of Jesus Christ on the cross to show forth His Love for His children. We are His priority. Will we embrace Him? His Love never fails. Everyone needs God's compassion and everyone needs His forgiveness; for it is through His forgiveness, His Love and through His compassion that the world will experience a better hope for salvation. Understanding God's design and accepting the principles can only be made at the cross on surrendered knees. These are God's priorities as set forth according to His precepts:

1. Our faithful relationship with the Lord.
2. Our dedication to our family.
3. Raising our children in the fear of the Lord.
4. Ministering in Love to our community.

The family is primarily our first ministry, followed by the duty to our community. The elders are called to minister within the churches, as mandated by God, but their first priority is to minister to their own families first before undertaking other roles. Understanding God's design for the family helps parents to understand God's purpose for the earthly family and also to understand the meaning of raising godly children: "… *train up a child the way he should go: and when he is old, he will not depart from it…*" (Proverbs 22:6, KJV). God expects the leader of the family to shepherd his assigned community, as he would shepherd his family and the church.

The family must be an example to the community, and in general to the world, dedicated to the service of the Lord. Yes, indeed, after the Lord, the family should be his first priority after service to the Lord, as revealed through the ministry of Jesus' Love for the family (Matthew 12:46–50): "*…let your light so shine before men, that they may see your good works and glorify your Father in heaven*" (Matthew 5:16, NKJV).

LOVE: THE MOST IMPORTANT RELATIONSHIP BETWEEN GOD AND MANKIND

Love reveals the wonder of God's creation as we study plants, animals and people. Love is a universal phenomenon that describes the indescribable gifts of God, and responds to relationship over religion. Love is the component on which Christ established His relationship on earth with man. Therefore, the most important relationship Adam had on earth prior to his fall was with God and with the host of heaven. Thus, this relationship was not based on any form of religion.

The relationship with God and mankind constitutes Love, accountability, leadership, and in essence, creates communication, fellowship and trustworthiness. It is not a relationship that is based on religious beliefs, but is based on the divine principles of Almighty God. Through abdication of his responsibility as king over the earth, Adam lost the most important relationship of all–the Holy Spirit. Through his violation of God's word, mankind was disqualified as God's representative on earth. According to Myles Munroe in *Rediscovering the Kingdom*: "Adam became an ambassador without portfolio, an envoy without official status, a citizen without a country, a king without a Kingdom, a ruler without a domain." That was the reason for the Holy Spirit's intimate relationship with mankind from the beginning.

God's dwelling presence with mankind, guaranteed communication and fellowship with the Holy Spirit as it reveals the purpose of God, on earth and in heaven, so that He could execute His will on earth. That was God's design for man. The intent of His original plan was to extend His rules, His power and His Kingdom on earth. His glorious desire was to manifest His character, wisdom, righteousness, and purpose through the administrative leadership of mankind in the world. Man was created, as noted, with God's ultimate goal of having the heavenly kingdom established on earth, with man as the ruler, just as it is in heaven so it would have been on earth. But Adam failed God by breaking His covenant.

The first earthly king Adam lost the Kingdom as a consequence of his rebellion against the Word of God; his duties were now performed by angels as he could no longer be trusted by the Lord. This however, serves as a reminder to those who are priests and kings that they too can lose their rights to gain access to the heavenly kingdom. Those who violate God's Law can and will be disqualified as representatives of the heavenly kingdom on earth.

Adam not only lost his personal relationship with his heavenly Father, but he also lost his position as God's representative to the earthly kingdom, and also the close relationship he once enjoyed with the Lord — a Love relationship. As a priest, king and leader of the earthly family, one must be careful not to lose sight of the rights, privilege and authority of such a high office, for the onus is on the leader to lead the family with Love and devotion, even as Christ Loves the church.

Adam lost the earthly kingdom. However, God's reaction to his defection and to his treacherous act was the promise that He made to the adversary, stating that:

> *I will put enmity between you and the woman, and between your offspring and her offspring; he shall bruise your head, and you shall bruise his heel. To the woman he said, "I will surely multiply your pain in childbearing; in pain you shall bring forth children. Your desire shall be for thy husband, and he shall rule over you."*
> —Genesis 3:15–16, ESV

It was the promise of a new offspring that broke the power of the adversary that would allow mankind to regain the authority and dominion that Adam once held. Through divine intervention, the earthly kingdom would be restored to the earthly family. This was the promise of God concerning the Messianic king and the return of the earthly kingdom to those for whom the Lord had prepared it.

As desired, the greatest need of mankind was restored. He thought he had lost his righteousness, rightly so, but the Lord had designed a new relationship, a new covenant through Jesus Christ, so that the earthly family might be restored to their earthly kingdom which the Lord had originally prepared for them. This is the purpose of God's redemptive program and restoration for mankind on earth when He returns. God will re-establish His kingdom on earth through the assignment of the Lord Jesus Christ, His Son. He will also restore the relationship that He once had with man. Since man's rebellion against his heavenly Father, God's plan was to redeem mankind back to himself, through the sacrifice of His Son Jesus Christ, which He did at the cross.

On this principle, God sent His only Son to redeem what had been lost in the Garden of Eden. There was no one greater than His Son Jesus Christ who could have restored the broken relationship that existed between the Lord and fallen man. Christ's relationship with mankind is the only element that could have been used as a catalyst to restore man's relationship with the heavenly Father. There was none worthy enough who could have repaired such broken relationship between mankind and the Father, except Jesus Christ, His Son. All were found guilty because of Adam's transgression.

If the present generation desires to pursue the restored relationship with God, without His Son, Jesus Christ, then it will not find Him. Because God requires that all should seek after Him only by faith, through Jesus Christ, it is a merited favor, based on our relationship with Him, through His Son. Instead of allowing us to wander in despair, loneliness and woe, He partnered with us, again, by the designing of a new righteous covenant, the sacrifice of His only begotten Son. Man's emptiness cannot be satisfied with earthly treasures and religious accolades, but only through his relationship with the Lord, through His Son, Jesus Christ.

A DESIRE FOR RELATIONSHIP

In His desire to enjoy a close relationship with His creation, God created mankind in His own image and placed in Him the ability to reason with Him as friend with friend. This gives mankind special access to the mind of God which He gave to no other creature on earth. It is with such blessedness that God placed His spirit within man, and man became a spirit with a physical body. With this spiritual body, God opened the window of communication, where He communicates with His creation. Through this wonderful plan, Adam was able to commune and fellowship with an infinite God even from the unseen realm, through the Spirit. The Lord imparted the knowledge, wisdom and understanding to Adam that allowed him to name his wife, Eve, and also allowed him to assign separate identities to every animal, plant and other living creatures. Adam's knowledge of all things created also allowed him to fellowship and to communicate with them all (Genesis 1 and 2). By this mankind could understand the Father's plans for both heaven and earth.

It is essential to understand also that before the foundation of the world and before the creation of mankind, the Love of God had existed. God's Love had existed before all things created, because it was out of His Love that He created man from the dust of the earth. God also instituted relationships, not just for the man, but also He continued His creative process by creating each animal in pairs. Nevertheless, He recognized that Adam was alone, and as a result, God created for him a helpmate, a woman, bone of his bones and flesh of his flesh, and Adam named her.

God's Love and provision for Adam at creation is a testimony to us all. In particular, God Loves us so much, even more than the birds of the air that He placed in us, His heavenly Spirit, which He imparted to no other creature (see Corinthians 2:4). There is definitely no one else like the Lord, who has given us the grace to do His will. He then continues to restore and to guide the earthly family into deeper interaction with Himself; as He responded to Adam's loneliness by providing for him a helpmate, a companion, desiring that he built a family structure, on earth, as an example for the generations which would come after. But Adam failed. Nevertheless, the will of the Lord must be done as He complemented Adam with a helpmate, instructing him that they should populate the earth, by creating a family structure on which the generations to follow will come to experience the Love of God through a new covenant.

With the restoration, the Lord promises to give us His grace to do His will. Our life is hidden in His plan and in His Love. It is God's promise that He will restore the soul of man from the sentence of death through a new generation, and through a new covenant by creating a new family structure, as He had done when He formed man from the dust of the earth and provided for him a mate. As He had done for Adam at the time of creation and at each time that He formed a new covenant, He will continue to do because He is determined that His will must be done on earth.

Many times believers stray from their relationship with God as they forget the covenant that comes with the relationship. Nevertheless, if believers would look back at creation when God created the earth, they would notice that it was after all things were created by the Lord and named by Adam that the Lord created for Adam a helpmate. God created Adam with desires and therefore He knew what the physical desire of the man would have been so God made for him a helpmate to fulfill certain physical needs. God is omniscient, yet He did not create Adam and Eve at the same together, but in His wisdom, He allowed Adam first to take responsibility of his position, for the Lord knew what the distraction of having a wife would have meant to Adam. Therefore, Adam's fleshly desire was the last to be fulfilled, when the Lord formed his wife Eve with bones taken from his ribs and presented her to Adam as his wife and helpmate.

In our journey with God, sometimes the waiting seems to be unbearable when it comes to making a choice in our personal companionship, as it does in opportunities within the secular world, and also in waiting for our healing (See Genesis 29:18–30). But, one thing is certain: God, the loving Father, will always provide the right opportunity, the right companion, and the right time for the healing power of His people. God's word states: *"...Seek ye first the Kingdom of God.. and all these things shall be added unto you..."* (Matthew 6:33, KJV).

"...the earth is the Lord's..." (Psalm 24:1, KJV) and he provides for His own and ensures that His people's needs are met; He provides comfort to those who are lonely; God will provide for His children. The Scripture declares:

> *The Lord is my Shepherd I shall not want. He maketh me to lie down in green pastures, He leadeth me besides still waters...He leadeth me in the paths of righteousness...*
> —Psalm 23:1–3, KJV

God knows our needs and He fulfills our desires. He knows when we are hungry; He knows when we are sad; He knows when we are hurting, and He also knows about those who have hurt us; He knows it all! However, His word declares that He will work everything out for our good. The struggles and the disappointments in our lives are the avenues that lead to the heart of the Lord.

If we were never sad, how would we know that He is a comforter? If we were never ill, how would we know that He is a healer? If we had never had problems, how would we know that He is the greatest problem solver of all? God is more than we could ever dream or imagine Him to be. The dying world needs to know this, that God will provide the perfect answers to their uncertainties. And this is His reason for creating the earthly family, that His Love may be established on earth.

According to the Word of God, we are commanded to "Comfort one another with these words" (1 Thessalonians 4:18, KJV). For those who are searching, there is no need to be misled by the deceptions of the enemy. Trust in the Lord and allow Him to guide your path. He will turn your sorrow into joy, and open doors that seem impossible. Remember: *"The earth is the Lord's, and the fullness thereof..."* (Psalm 24:1, KJV). The Lord will never allow dishonor to befall His glorious name. As a true testament of God's Love, David testifies when he states: *"I have been young, and now am old, yet have I not seen the righteous forsaken, nor their seed begging bread,"* (Psalm 37:25, KJV).

In our experience and in sharing the joy and the Love of God, we must also show virtue and patience to those around us. Yes, the Lord is a God of His word; He declares it and it is done: 'Let there be…" and everything submits to His command. Also, the Lord is a God of structure and order. There is a time and a season for everything. God's delay in His response to our request is by no means a denial to us, but at times, God is working out His purpose for our greater good, greater than what our eyes can behold.

In delivering the children of Israel from the hand of their enemy, God sent His guiding angel ahead of their enemy's army to ensure the safety of His people, before they crossed over (Exodus 33:2). But what if the Lord had sent the children of Israel on their way with their enemies leading them? The same can be said for today in the secular world. The Lord will not allow His people to be led by those who do not know Him. The Lord is our keeper therefore He will continue to guide us in the path that He has chosen for us. He will not remain silent, but He will guide us through situations for our learning. Nevertheless, those who do not understand will question their situation. Jesus' disciples asked, when they saw the blind man, *"…who did sin…?"* (John 9:2, KJV).

Nevertheless as we go through our different struggles and trials, the work of God will manifest. We will learn to reach out to the Lord and to develop a more intimate relationship with Him. We will also learn how to be better stewards of our earthly gifts, so that when promotion comes (and it will come, because the work of God has manifested itself through us), as a result, everyone will be able to see and identify the Love of God in us.

This manifestation of God's Love will draw others to us. We sometimes fail to recognize the glory of God around us, however, there is always something indescribable about those who are called by His name and are led by His Spirit. When the Love of God is within us, our lives will bear witness, so that the unbelievers will come to know Him.

We must never forget who we are: we are children of the Most High God and we are of the royal household. We are blessed, and we are the called and chosen children of the Lord. Therefore, let us declare it and let the adversary know that we are going to inflict the Love of God on the people of the world by living according to God's plan.

In examining God's relationship with mankind, we will discover God's intended purpose for His creation. Before Jesus came, God's Love for us was already initiated in His master plan. This is the inherent nature of the Lord's Love on which He established the sacred covenant of marriage between the man and the woman.

A LOVING DESIGN

We were 'fearfully and wonderfully' created by the loving hand of God. As the Psalmist declares: "*I will praise thee; for I am fearfully and wonderfully made: marvelous are thy works; and that my soul knows right well*" (Psalm 139:14, KJV). This Psalmist gives a descriptive view of God's creative power through His Love. In God we were created with the features to reflect His magnificent Love and His holy character. It is through this creative power that God identifies Himself with us, as through His Son Jesus who became sin for us. As the Scripture states: "*He was despised and rejected by mankind, a man of suffering, and familiar with pain*" (Isaiah 53:3b, NIV).

God, through Jesus, identifies Himself with us through His death on the cross. Love is the center of God's heart for His creation. On this foundation, He established His commandments throughout the Old and New Covenants. It was through this same principle that John, His beloved Apostle experienced the revelation of God's Love (John 3:16). As a result of his relationship with Jesus, scholars now call him, "The Beloved of Christ."

Through this ultimate expression, reveals the highest manifestation of God's Love by the life, the crucifixion, and the resurrection of Jesus Christ.

Before the institution of the Church, the Lord created the family; through the family, He instituted the covenant of marriage, and now we are the product of His creative power.

We were created to perform His will on earth through the family unit. Understanding who we are can only be materialized if and when we are ready to return to our 'First Love', who is the Lord, the Creator of all things. We are God's masterpiece designed with His abounding Love.

WALK THROUGH

Dear Father,

I need You. I acknowledge that I have been directing my own life and that, as a result, I have sinned against You. I thank You that You have forgiven my sins through Christ's death on the cross for me.

Nothing matters more to me than my Love for You and for my family, and also for my community. My family is very important to me, and in my daily fellowship with my family, I have discovered more about You, dear Lord. I have chosen this day to remain in Your Love and to become better connected with You, through spiritual devotion with my family in the spirit of Love, appreciation and honor, relying on Your divine guidance.

Amen.

SUMMARY AND REFLECTION

True or False? God's calling for our lives was not to marry the person we Love, but to Love the person we marry. _____

Complete the following:

God's design for the family are _____ in the root of Love, strictly because, God is the ever _____ theme in the Bible. Of all the other books, the Bible is the only book of _____.

When we become fragmented emotionally, spiritually and intellectually, it is a sign that we have lost the _____ and _____ of family commitments.

Name two out of the four purposes God created the family to accomplish

a) _____
b) _____

True or False? Family roles are sometimes based a family traditions.

_____

Complete the following:

How important is it to the Lord that we not experience loneliness, and why did He create us as a pair, man and woman? _____

_____

God wants us to become enlightened, not only in the satisfaction of our personal life, but in all dimensions of the total person which are:

a) _____

b) _____

c) _____

d) _____

e) _____

Evaluation And Temperament

Complete the two-part question:

1. If you find yourself tempted by competing desires to stray outside of your marriage, which approach do you think you should take to deal with the situation?

    a) Moderate (take no action)
    b) Temperamental Approach (withdrawn emotionally)
    c) Assertive (aggressive steps to deal with issues)
    d) Prayerful (guidance and wisdom)
    e) Compulsive Analytic (alter your emotion to discern)

2. An active part of children's upbringing is the responsibility of both parents. Which two of the following statements describe how it should be?

    a) The father's greater responsibility is to ensure that his family is spiritually protected from ungodly influences of the world.

    b) Spiritually, it is the father's responsibility and maturely it is the mother's; she carries a cradle of Love, patience and understanding.

    c) Both parents are responsible for the nurturing of their children. The father who is the priest of the family must be patient and nurturing, ensuring that discipline is conducive to the will of the Lord.

    d) The nurturing of the children is a responsibility that the Lord has placed on the shoulders of both parents. Responsibilities pointing to the biblical commands make the leadership of the head of the household more demanding.

    e) The process of parenting is the task of both parents

3. What has Jesus revealed to you that will have an impact on your Love and appreciation for your family? _____

_____

4. To become successful in relationship with our children, we should:

  a) Seek to work toward providing a good model of Christ-like behavior, by redefining our interest, our patience and our understanding in a godly manner.

  b) Demonstrate emotional vulnerabilities and learn to express honest weakness and immaturity.

  c) Control our emotions but express honesty when caught in weakness and immature behavior.

  d) Aim at damaging the child's sense of self-esteem and defeat any lasting relationship with peers in building a biblical value system.

  e) Do not attempt to create crisis; do not praise superficial characters.

  f) Do not damage a child's sense of value, or self-worth as it will defeat any lasting relationship with peers, and inhibit his/her biblical values.

5. After reading this first chapter, which two of the following lessons will impact most profoundly on your devotion to God and will reflect more positively on your spiritual, social and physical life, as they relate to the content of Love and leadership in your family and towards others?

  a) As one learns to understand the frailty of his responsibilities and of God's continuous Love and forgiveness, it leads him through a measure of development that defines who he is in God and who he can be to his family.

  b) This is humbling and challenging, but it is also a privilege and a great responsibility to serve the Lord and to perform His will on earth with courage and humility.

  c) Embracing the responsibility with faith is encouraging and therefore will make life more rewarding for you and your family.

d) My responsibility can either be a success or a failure depending on my spiritual pursuit of maturity in Christ.

e) I am moved to increase my Christ-likeness spirit in order to maintain a greater family bonding in the home and becoming a chain breaker against family struggles.

f) Seriously considering just how important my responsibilities and consequences are to God and my family.

6. Whenever we get too busy to spend time in fellowship with the Word and with our family, it is most likely a result of:

a) Lacking the understanding concerning family relationship and the responsibility as it relates to marriage.

b) Weakness in spiritual leadership as we ought to Love our family regardless of the difficulties that we may be faced with.

c) The desire to fulfill the lust of the flesh, thus hindering spiritual growth, which then encourages physical and emotional disconnect within the family.

d) Not committed to the discovery of the truth, while at the same time, not living by the godly principles that will protect, empower and govern the life of the family.

e) Not being a true disciple of Christ, and not seeing this as a priority to grow and mature in Love towards God and towards the family.

7. Write down three goals and expectations that are crucial to building a lifetime relationship with the Lord.

Goal 1:

_____

_____

_____

_____

Goal 2:

_____

_____

_____

_____

Goal 3:

_____

_____

_____

_____

8. Husbands: Choose the most passionate way in which you should Love your wife and then write down what inspires this aspect of your Love for her.

a) Love her more passionately because of the inspiration I received from reading this book?

_____

_____

_____

b) Love her because it is a requirement for holy life of Christ's revelation in you towards her?

_____

_____

_____

c) Love her through the revealed Love of Christ?

_____

_____

_____

d) Love her because of who she is to me, and to my children, and because of her Love for the Lord?

_____

_____

_____

e) Love your wife because of her compassion for others and for the church?

_____

_____

_____

9. Do you Love your wife, even as Christ Loves the Church?

   a) Spiritually yes
   b) Partially there
   c) Fairly yes
   d) Relationally yes

LOVE REQUEST

Things that are missing from your life and that you would like to experience that would make you at peace with yourself, or most importantly understanding what the will of God is in relation to the lesson.

> *"Search me oh Lord and know my thoughts I pray, try me and see if..."*
>
> —Psalm 139:23, NIV

Write down three words of the Love that you would like to see manifested, reaffirmed and resolved in your life, your family and in the lives of your friends.

_____

_____

_____

Please send this Love request to my prayer request ministry via email and we will be glad to supplicate with you before God, our mediator and great intercessor.

Love Reveals the Heart of God!

Darkness cannot drive out darkness: only light can do that. Hate cannot drive out hate: only Love can do that.

— Martin Luther King Jr.

My message... were not with wise and persuasive words,
but with a demonstration of the Spirit's power,
so that your faith might not rest on human wisdom, but on
God's power.

—1 Corinthians 2:4–5, NIV

And this I pray, that your love may abound still
more and more in real knowledge and all discernment.

—Philippians 1:9, NASB

CHAPTER TWO

True Discernment Is Expressed In Love

rue discernment when expressed in Love is aligned with the peace of God's anointing. As the Word of God declares,

> ... *the wisdom from above is first of all pure. It is also peace loving, gentle at all times, and willing to yield to others. It is full of mercy and good deeds. It shows no favoritism and is always sincere.*
> —James 3:17, NLT

The insight and discernment that come from God is motivated through Love, and it is built on the foundation of the indwelling presence and peace of God.

The characteristics of true discernment are seen and experienced as persons operate under the prophetic gifts of the Holy Spirit. This then results in the form of good leadership that is welcoming, warm, and is uplifting for the family of Christ. Such characteristics place the ministry in a position for positive growth, as well as for the opening of channels for spiritual discernment. Likewise, it encourages the response of individuals to the call for repentance which further fulfills the mandate of God by bringing souls to repentance, as they are being born into the Kingdom of God.

> *To Clearly Hear the Voice of the Lord,*
> *Individuals Need to Have the Indwelling Peace*
> *Abiding in Their Hearts.*

The fruit of peace should be resonating in the heart of all believers if it is their desire to intimately commune with the Lord. According to James 3: 18: *"And the fruit of righteousness is sown in peace of them that make peace"* (James 3:18, KJV). It is through the spirit of peace and fellowship that believers will be able to spread God's Love to the unbelievers, as they share the joy of their anointed experience with them: the experience which brings believers closer together, without jealousy, strife, or an unforgiving and hateful heart. James 4:1 declares: *"From whence come wars and fightings among you? come they not hence, even of your lusts that war in your members?"* (James 4:1, KJV)

One of the four principles that the early Christians in the book of Acts, were able to devote themselves to was the close fellowship among the saints. Fellowship was one of their primary reasons for their continued worshipping together. Except for the ministering of the Holy Ghost, fellowship was the most important element of the growth of the early Church, and one of the things that had the most positive effect on the life of the Corinthian Christians. We should not be surprised, then, that the early Church had experienced such massive outpouring of revival. *"They devoted themselves to the apostles' teachings and to fellowship, to the breaking of bread and to prayer"* (Acts 2:42, NIV). Luke tells us that they devoted themselves to fellowship. They were not only congregating in one place, but their reason for coming together was to worship the Lord as one body of believers. The Corinthian Christians, made the worshipping of the Lord their ministry's main priority:

> But if we keep living in the light as He himself is in the light, we have fellowship with one another, and the blood of Jesus His Son cleanses us from all sin.
>
> —1 John 1:7, ISV

> And they continued stedfastly in the apostles' doctrine and fellowship, and in breaking of bread, and in prayers.
>
> —Acts: 2:42, KJV

> Let us not give up meeting together, as some are in the habit of doing, but encouraging one another—and all the more as you see the Day approaching.
>
> —Hebrews 10:25, NIV

The New Covenant, in this dispensation cannot be likened to that of the Old Testament Covenant, because with the Old Covenant, which was the Jewish law, had no power to forgive sin. According to the Apostle Paul to the Galatians saints,

> *Now before faith came, we were held captive under the law, imprisoned until the coming faith would be revealed. So then, the law was our guardian until Christ came, in order that we might be justified by faith. But now that faith has come, we are no longer under a guardian...*
>
> —Galatians 3:23-25, ESV

Also, as noted by the Apostle Paul to the Hebrew saints, "*Anyone who has set aside the Law of Moses dies without mercy on the evidence of two or three witnesses*" (Hebrew 10:28, ESV). The people of God, during the Old Testament Covenant period, were not able to commune directly with the Lord; they were made to go through the office of the High Priest, to whom they would confess their sins, after which the High Priest would take their petitions and their offerings of animal sacrifice to the Lord on their behalf for the forgiveness of their sins.

But now, under the New Testament Covenant, through the death, burial and resurrection of Jesus Christ, the ritual of the high priest seeking forgiveness on behalf of the people of God has been abolished. Now forgiveness is by faith through Jesus Christ our Lord.

> *For where a testament is, there must also of necessity be the death of the testator. For a testament is of force after men are dead: otherwise it is of no strength at all while the testator liveth.*
>
> —Hebrews 9:16-17, KJV

Under the New Covenant, believers have now gained access to boldly approach the throne of God without fear or condemnation. As Paul states: "*There is therefore now no condemnation to them who are in Christ Jesus*" (Romans 8:1, ESV). Except for our own stubborn will, we can never be separated from God's Love and mercy. Paul asks: "*Who shall separate us from the Love of Christ? Shall tribulation...nakedness, or danger or sword?*" (Romans 8:35, ESV) The Lord in mercy sent His Son to be the sacrificial lamb for our sins, when the blood of goats and bullocks and the office of the high priest were no longer effective in man's redemption. As the Word of God justly states: *"For God so loved the world that he gave his only Son, that whoever believes in him shall not perish, but have eternal life"* (John 3:16, NIV).

The Old Testament Covenant was instituted by the Lord in order that He might reveal to His people the standards of righteousness by which the relationship with Him should be governed. It was also meant to provide the rules of conduct for the Old Covenant period, which the people had proven that they were not able to live by. But, in His grace and mercy, the Lord sent His only Son, Jesus Christ, to bear our sins and to replace the harshness of the Old Covenant.

With this New Covenant, Jesus brought grace and mercy through His death on the cross. The New Covenant affords us the privilege of personally taking our petitions to the Lord, thus enabling us to enter into the presence of the Lord without the fear of condemnation and without the fear of death as we present our petitions before Him. In His presence, we are now able to listen to His still small voice as we plead our case to Him and as we kneel before His righteous throne of grace.

> *But Christ came as a high priest of the good things to come... Not through the blood of goats and calves, but through His own blood ... For if the blood of goats and bulls and the ashes of a heifer, sprinkling those who have been defiled sanctify for the cleansing of the flesh, how much more shall the blood of Christ, who through the eternal Spirit offered Himself without blemish to God, cleanse your conscience from dead works to serve the living God? For this reason he is the mediator of a new covenant since a death has taken place for the redemption of the transgressions that were committed under the first covenant, those who have been called may receive the promise of the eternal inheritance. For where a covenant is, there must of necessity be the death of the one who made it. For a covenant is valid only when men are dead, for it is never in force while the one who made it lives. Therefore even the first covenant was not inaugurated without blood. For when every commandment had been spoken by Moses to all the people according to the Law, he took the blood of the calves and the goats, with water and scarlet wool and hyssop, and*

sprinkled both the book itself and all the people, saying, 'This is the blood of the covenant which God has commanded you.'
—*Hebrews 9:11–20, NASB*

The Lord Jesus has demonstrated the true meaning of Love, which all believers must strive to emulate. The spirit of Love must be the essential theme of the Church. It should be the driving force behind the structure of the organization and the positive embodiment of all congregational leaders. When the Love of Jesus is present within the Church, it enables the spirit of transformation, as it brings spiritual guidance and holy revival into the Body of Christ.

True discernment does not rest upon human wisdom, neither does it rest on the excellence of speech or on any physiological discoveries (James 3:13–17). This is accomplished only through the principles taught at the altar of prayer, in the believers' faith and in fasting. True discernment is also achieved through the daily studying of the Word of the Lord, and also through the continued presentation of one's self at the throne of grace.

If any of you lacks wisdom, let him ask of God, who gives to all liberally and without reproach, and it will be given to him. But let him ask in faith, with no doubting, for he who doubts is like a wave of the sea driven and tossed by the wind. For let not that man suppose that he will receive anything from the Lord; he is a double-minded man, unstable in all his ways.
—James 1:5–8, NKJV

The true discernment is recognized as heavenly wisdom (James 3:17). It is that special ability that God gives to members of the Body of Christ who are able to discern the differences between pure motives and the impurity of thoughts, between holiness and the things that are profane. The discerner must be able to identify the presence of godly actions and evil doings. It is important also for the believers to be led by the Spirit of the Lord, by His guidance and through His willingness to intercede in prayer, on behalf of others as he communes daily with the Lord through the Holy Ghost.

Her priests have violated My Law and profaned My holy things;
they have not distinguished between the holy and unholy, nor have
they made known the difference between the unclean and the clean;
and they have hidden their eyes from My Sabbaths, so that I am
profaned among them.

—Ezekiel 22:26, NKJV

Those who are empowered with the gift of discernment should be
held to the highest standard of spiritual integrity within the church. These
are persons who should be empowered with the offices of counselors, pastors, Bible teachers, spiritual advisors and church elders (1 Kings 3:16–28,
Ephesians 4:11–14 and Acts 1:22–26). These individuals must be spiritually
insightful, sensitive and decisive in their approach towards those who are
entrusted to their care; their wisdom and their judgment cannot be compro-
mised, and should be in accordance with that of Solomon's wisdom. Their
heart must be yearning with compassion for those who are broken and are
in despair. In the courtroom of righteous justice, wisdom, knowledge and
understanding must be working in unison to accomplish the plan of God.

The woman whose son was living spoke to the king [King Solomon],
for she yearned with compassion for her son; and she said, "O my
lord, give her the living child and by no means kill him!" But the oth-
er said, "Let him be neither mine nor yours, but divide him." So the
king answered and said, "Give the first woman the living child, and
by no means kill him; she is his mother." And all Israel heard of the
judgment which the king had rendered; and they feared the king, for
they saw that the wisdom of God was in him to administer justice.

—1 Kings 3:26–28, NKJV

Those who operate under the gift of discernment must possess the
ability to identify the differences between compulsive and spiritual anointing, which are revealed through the Holy Spirit. These are important components of this ministry, because misunderstanding of the operation of
the Holy Spirit by non-believers or by immature Christians can become
serious hindrances to the growth of the ministry. We must not encourage
the spirit of fear, the spirit of anger, or the spirit of intimidation to take
precedence over the spirit of boldness and Love. Instead, we must express

the truth in Love as we are guided by the Holy Spirit. True discernment will be accompanied with signs and wonders and under the anointing of the power of the Lord.

> *Every good and perfect gift is from above, coming down from the Father of the heavenly lights, who does not change like shifting shadows.*
> —James 1:17, NIV

> *These are the miraculous signs that will accompany believers: They will use the power and authority of my name to force demons out of people. They will speak new languages.*
> —Mark 16: 17, GWT

> *Where there is no vision the people perish.*
> —Proverbs 29:18, KJV

The Bible records the mystery of God that was hidden from mankind, including His power, wisdom, and glory. This was the Lord's plan from the beginning of creation, to defeat the devices of Satan. Through this mysterious act of the Almighty, He qualifies us as subjects and citizens to His Kingdom. In that, we are officially and legally sons and joint-heirs in God's Kingdom – a new name! Ephesians declares:

> *That the Lord Jesus Christ, the Father of glory, may give unto you the spirit of wisdom and revelation in the knowledge of him. The eyes of your understanding being enlightened; that ye may know what is the hope of his calling, and what the riches of the glory of his inheritance in the saints; And what is the exceeding greatness of his power to us-ward who believe, according to the working of his mighty power, Which he wrought in Christ, when he raised him from the dead, and set him at his own right hand in the heavenly places, Far above all principality, and power, and might, and dominion, and every name that is named, not only in this world, but also in that which is to come; And hath put all things under his feet, and gave him to be the head over all things to the church, which is his body, the fullness of him that filleth all in all.*
> —Ephesians 1:17–22, KJV

But we are citizens of heaven, where the Lord Jesus Christ lives. And we are eagerly waiting for him to return as our Savior.
—Philippians 3:20, NLT

During Jesus' ministry on earth, only a certain portion of God's glory was revealed, which only shed light on the plan of God for us. According to the writer of Ephesians, there has been a penitent desire of man for change or deliverance since creation. Nevertheless, since Jesus had already been predestined according to prophecy to be the sacrificial lamb for man's redemption, God could not go back on His Word. God cannot lie. As the Psalmist confidently declares: "*Forever, O LORD, Your Word is settled in heaven*" (Psalm 119:89, NASB) and "*I will declare that your love stands firm forever, that you have established your faithfulness in heaven itself*" (Psalm 89:2, NIV).

On the same principle of the Word of God, Jesus boldly asked: "… *But whom say ye that I am? …and Peter answereth and saith unto him, Thou art the Christ*" (Mark 16:16, KJV). "*But the Word of the Lord stands forever.*" *And this is the Word that was preached to you*" (1Peter 1:25, NIV).

The Lord, through His word, reveals the hidden mystery of His plan for our lives, through the death, burial, and resurrection of His Son Jesus Christ according to the revelation of Paul, as stated in Romans: the purpose of God's mystery was to transform and enlighten those who are eagerly awaiting the wonders and signs of God, as:

…To the intent that now the manifold wisdom of God might be made known by the church to the principalities and powers in the heavenly places; According to the eternal purpose which He accomplished in Christ Jesus our Lord; In whom we have boldness and access with confidence through faith in Him.
—Ephesians 3:10–12, NKJV

Beforehand, the Levitical law could not have continued as it only foreshadowed the greater power that was to come which would fulfill the law of the new dispensation of grace through the death, burial and resurrection of Jesus Christ.

Saul understood the law of the prophets but after he experienced the voice of God on the road called straight, his life was completely transformed from hatred to humility. On this affirmation, his name changed from Saul to Paul. With such transformation, he declared the Word of God to the Gentiles through the inspiration of the Holy Spirit. Upon such conviction he was able to instruct the saints with these words:

"For the law of the Spirit of life in Christ Jesus has set you free from the law of sin and of death" (Romans 8:2, NASB).

Jesus said:

> *Don't misunderstand why I have come. I did not come to abolish the Law of Moses or the writings of the prophets. No, I came to accomplish their purpose.*
>
> —Matthew 5:17, NLT

Paul's encounter with God had enabled him to support his writing to the Gentiles in conjunction with the law of the Torah and above all, with the Love of God. Paul never wrote of his own knowledge, even though he was a learned student under the ministry of his master Gamaliel. Upon that authority, he declares these words: *"Love does no wrong to others, so love fulfills the requirements of God's law"* (Romans 13:10, NLT).

On Christ the solid rock, Paul also declares the hope of knowing Christ in these words:

> *"For the whole Law is fulfilled in one word, in the statement, '... You shall love your neighbor as yourself.'*
>
> —Galatians 5:14, NASB

The gift of discernment is to be used with Love and compassion. Peter and his brothers went fishing; they toiled all night and caught nothing; Jesus saw their plight, and in the spirit of compassion and discernment, He said to them: *"Cast the net on the right side of the boat..."* (John 21:6, ESV). Their boat and their net were immediately filled with fish as they obeyed His instructions. Many believers miss their blessing because they are not in tuned to the divine will of God for their lives. They hear His words but they do not obey them, even though they know that the Lord expects them to be obedient to His command. Let us not forget that Peter was faithful being a fisherman. He demonstrates that one can still muster strength despite doubt and personal struggles. In fact, such struggles may demonstrate proof of the miraculous in Peter's faith and obedience in Christ Jesus; this is possible in our life too. As with Peter and his brothers, it was not their gifts that qualified them for ministry; instead it was their humility and submissive spirit to Jesus' command.

When Israel was defeated by the Syrian army, Elisha, the man of God, instructed King Joash to shoot his arrow through the east window, *"the arrow of the Lord's deliverance, and the arrow of deliverance from Syria"* (2 Kings 13:17, KJV). He then told King Joash to strike the ground. King Joash hit the ground only three times and stopped. Elisha told him when he stopped that if he had continued he would have fully defeated his enemies (2 Kings 13:12–19). Here again is illustrated that where complete obedience to God's instructions are not carried out, the greatest reward will not be achieved.

Successful leaders are the ones who are able to impart the Love of God, to show temperance and who are also able to spiritually discern the true gift of the Holy Spirit. In the feeding of the five thousand people who were following Him, Jesus discerned their needs with compassion. The word of God states: *"…When it was evening, the disciples came to him, saying… '…the day is now over; send the crowds away to…buy food for themselves"* (Matthew 14:15, ESV). The disciples wanted Jesus to send the people back to their homes so that they could be fed because the disciples lacked the spirit of discernment. The behavior of the disciples clearly demonstrated that they were not able to understand the power that Jesus had, even though they had seen the many miracles that He had performed.

Spiritual leaders, especially when they are called upon to minister to those who seek their spiritual guidance, must be empowered with the spiritual gift of compassion. They must be prayerfully ready at all times to demonstrate godly leadership qualities that embody the Love of God. It is understandable, though, that sometimes in times of crisis, many will lose their faith and become frustrated. Like the disciples, they are not always able to demonstrate the strength of faith, the embodiment of compassion and the joy of Love. However, this lack of godly attributes ought not to be found among those who are called upon to be leaders of those who seek their spiritual guidance. The lack of godly attributes among spiritual leaders will have negative effects among unbelievers, thus hindering them from the path of righteousness.

Can souls be won for the Kingdom if spiritual leaders lack the spiritual wisdom to lead? Jesus demonstrated the perfect attributes of leadership qualities when He was faced with chaotic situations. In the situation where He had five thousand hungry people and no food to feed them, His compassion and mercy went above and beyond human understanding of Love.

The power of discernment expressed in Love will always bring connection and confirmation of the divine will of God. A little boy came to Jesus with two fish and five loaves of bread. The question has been asked "Could it be that, the little boy felt Jesus' heart?" Yes, many do believe this to be the case. The power of discernment expressed in Love can only transmit Love in confirmation with the Holy Spirit, as stated in 1 Corinthians 13: The Love-connection transferred from Jesus' heart to the little boy's heart was so remarkable that it changed the lives of many people on that day.

Love will imitate Love. Love knows no other affection than itself. In fact, Love cannot operate outside of its parameters. It has to be in an environment of kindness and gentleness. The gifts of the Spirit are only governed by true Love and are also only communicated through Love. Love is one of the nutrients that enriches and empowers the gifts of the Spirit to grow against hatred, jealousy and survive. As a result of its qualities, Love is always pure, Love is unselfish and Love motivates spiritual gifts. The word of the Lord declares: *"When I see the blood, I will pass over you"* (Exodus 12:13, NLT)–this means that we are untouchable! The word of God also says, *"Love covers a multitude of sins"* (1 Peter 4:8, TLB). I believe both of these covenants cover us. The blood and the Love of Jesus both protect God's people from the power of the prince of this world.

> *Godly discernment is agreeing with the heart of God,*
> *operating in Love, grace and humility.*

The Love of God conquers all and the blood of Jesus covers all, meaning, therefore, that the blood of Jesus is the embodiment of the power of God's Love for His people. This should not be misinterpreted that we as God's people do not have the responsibility to demonstrate the same power of Love one towards another. The revelation that we need Jesus also reveals that, as His people, we also need the Love of one another.

It is through accepting Jesus that we will experience and know the true meaning of Love. After all, it was Love that sent Jesus to the cross to die for our sins. The child with the two fish and five loaves of bread felt

Jesus' Love and compassion for the hungry crowd and responded immediately. Love searches the deepest sea and the darkest valley to discover its
hidden secrets. It reaches out to those who are in need. Love looks beyond
the faults of our neighbors and reaches out to them in their time of need.
"*This poor man cried and the Lord heard him*" (Psalm 34:6, NIV). As we cry,
Jesus will discern our needs. He understands every pain that we endure.

The counsel of God is also another example that is based on true discernment. They work together with one accord, confirming and with one
specific aim. There are various examples in the Scriptures that reveal the
true characteristics of discernment as expressed in Love.

1. Conspiracy vs. Discernment: Nehemiah discerned the plot
   of his enemies and refused to run away.

   One day I went to the house of Shemaiah son of Delaiah,
   the son of Mehetabel, who was shut in at his home. He said,
   "Let us meet in the house of God, inside the temple, and
   let us close the temple doors, because men are coming to kill
   you—by night they are coming to kill you." But I said,
   "Should a man like me run away? Or should someone like
   me go into the temple to save his life? I will not go!" I realized that God had not sent him, but that he had prophesied against me because Tobiah and Sanballat had hired him.
   He had been hired to intimidate me so that I would commit
   a sin by doing this, and then they would give me a bad name
   to discredit me. Remember Tobiah and Sanballat, because of
   what they have done; remember also the prophet Noadiah
   and how she and the rest of the prophets have been trying to
   intimidate me. So the wall was completed on the twenty-fifth
   of Elul, in fifty-two days. (Nehemiah 6:10–14, NIV)

2. The woman at the well—A reflection of the Father's heart
   in the gift of discernment, along with wisdom and compassion (John 4:4, 16–19).

3. In the Temple Court, Jesus accurately discerned the motives
   and thoughts of the teachers of the Law (John 8).

4. Simon Peter speaks by the Spirit of God and Jesus discerned this was not flesh and blood but by the Holy Ghost (Matthew 16:16–17).

5. Peter influenced by Satan—Jesus discerned and rebuked the spirit of illusion (Matthew 16:22–23).

6. Paying of Taxes to Caesar—Jesus discerned their true motives on the question (Matthew 22:15–18).

7. The heart of Nathaniel—Jesus discerned the pureness of his heart as a true Israelite (John 1:47–50).

8. Ruling and Government—We see evidence of discernment and wisdom in the life of Joseph and Pharaoh (Genesis 41:39–40).

The spirit of God knows all things, even the very deep things of man. He searches the hearts as expressed in Psalm 139. He knows our very thought patterns because His Spirit lives in each person. No one can know what's in the heart of a man except he says it, or it is revealed by the Holy Spirit. In the same way, no one knows the thoughts of God except the Spirit of God. What we have received is not the spirit of the world but the Spirit of God, who is of God. Therefore, we can understand what God has freely given us through the sacrifice of His Son, Jesus Christ. As a result of this awesome experience and glory, many have generated their own meaning and interpretation of the evidence of Christ. This is why the natural man will never understand the revelation of the Spirit for they are spiritually blind and the things of God are hidden from him.

This is also the very essence of why we must be in constant prayer, because we are constantly fighting a spiritual warfare. Because we are fighting a spiritual battle, we need the Spirit of the Lord to guide us through the battles.

Leaders who lack the spirit of discernment are more apt to make snap judgment concerning spiritual things, because the mind of Christ is not being nurtured through prayer and fasting. They have not discovered the mind of Christ. The Spirit of Christ reveals the heart of Christ. It is also here that the spirit of discernment is developed as it enlightens and reveals the heart of Christ to those who seek Him. Without the directions of the Spirit of God, leaders will not be able to get the revelation of the heart of God.

It takes the Holy Spirit to reveal the content of the heart. In order to operate in the Spirit, the believer's heart has to be transformed. The inner and outer veils that would normally cover the heart must first be removed. This will then allow the believers to be seen by the world, as Christ is to be seen. We can only discern the motives of others when the Spirit of God reveals the intent of their heart to the discerners. The motives of what is in the heart will be expressed in Love. Out of the heart *"flow the issues of life"* (Proverbs 4:23, JUB).

TRUE DISCERNMENT WILL EXPRESS TRUTH IN LOVE

True discernment cannot be derived from foreknowledge or driven by human perception. According to James, 1:17, the gift of discernment is without partiality even if the person is not genuine. The spirit of Love in us should overlook the bad in a person, or better yet, pick the positive out of the negative. Therefore, as one discerns in Love, he or she should allow the Holy Spirit to do the inward purification and not us. Many times we do the judging of the person ourselves even when they have good traits. Lastly, we should not change the revelation of the Holy Spirit about the person whether he is our friend or not, since the spirit of God does not lie.

You cannot react to what you see, hear or think, and call it true discernment. Neither is true discernment "pent up feelings" or "hearsay" that is unfortunately used in some preaching, teaching, and even prophesying. True discernment is allowing the Holy Spirit to reveal the truth in Love and forgiveness with the right attitude. In fact, true discernment is developed spiritually as we grow in Love.

The more spiritually developed we are, the more spiritually sound and mature we will become. Spiritual maturity makes way for the administration of the gift or gifts of the Holy Spirit, which manifest in a prosperous way, empowering the Church. This is because, as spiritual maturity takes place, our attitude, perception and likeness in Christ take on a different meaning. Our approach becomes Christ-minded, forgiving and compassionate. Our spiritual perception becomes enlightened and the hearts of others become transparent as the inner man is constantly maturing in the word of God:

For this very reason, make every effort to add to your faith goodness; and to goodness, knowledge; and to knowledge, self-control; and to self-control, perseverance; and to perseverance, godliness; and to godliness, mutual affection; and to mutual affection, love. For if you possess these qualities in increasing measure, they will keep you from being ineffective and unproductive in your knowledge of our Lord Jesus Christ. But whoever does not have them is nearsighted and blind, forgetting that they have been cleansed from their past sins.
—1 Peter 1:5-9, NIV

Spiritual discernment will increase as we learn to listen attentively to the voice of the Holy Spirit. It is important to be spiritually balanced as it will act as a shield to the doctrines of the devils and the wind of heresies. Additionally, growth will take place in our spiritual life if we can control the influence of the flesh, the mind of self and negative gainsayers. Never attempt to resolve spiritual events using physical means of experience (i.e. book counseling). Jesus will never reveal the hearts of men to you when you are driven by your own impulsive reaction. The person who walks in forgiveness will not walk in deception. Sadly, people who walk in deception or contrariness often believe that they have the gift of discernment. They truly believe that they are hearing from God, even when they are hurting their brothers and sisters. The truth of the matter is the person who is contrary and easily tossed by every wind of doctrine and manifestation is not a discerner. A discerner cannot be compulsive or too analytical, but rather be prudent and prayerful in each approach. Jesus says we are to try the Spirit. Solomon says, *"If you talk a lot, you are sure to sin; if you are wise, you will keep quiet"* (Proverbs 10:19, NCV). Therefore the bottom line is that discernment is not about imagination, a good guess, or last night's dream. It is about seeking counsel from God, recognizing God's way.

THE SECRET TO TRUE DISCERNMENT

True discernment cannot be derived from the knowledge of man's thoughts neither can it be achieved out of human perception. If something is spiritually discerned, it must be genuinely revealed through the power of the Holy Spirit and through genuine Love and compassion, as revelation, manifestation and confirmation (Acts 3; 16:16–19). A leader cannot react to what is seen, to what is disclosed to him by others or by what he perceived through his own thoughts, as these cannot be interpreted as true spiritual discernment. True discernment is revealed through the apparatus of living and walking in the spirit of the Word and the fruit of righteousness. Unfortunately, the lack of true spiritual discernment can sometimes cause spiritual leaders to lose sight of the divine will of the Lord, thus they prophesy under the guise of their own thoughts.

Real and true discernment is allowing the Holy Spirit to reveal the truth in Love, thus with the offer of forgiveness combined with an attitude of patience. True discernment is acquired spiritually as we grow in Love, which is the fruit of God's Love, as stated in Galatians chapter 5. The more spiritually developed we become, the more spiritually mature we will become. Spiritual maturity makes way for the administration of the gifts of the Holy Spirit, which manifests in the spiritual empowerment of the leadership of the church. Thus, the only way to grow is to love and by loving through leading, the fruit of Christ makes us more Christ-like and seasoned with the grace of maturity.

As spiritual maturity develops our attitude, our perception and our likeness in Christ Jesus become more meaningful, which is the true result of justification. Our approach to the dealing of spiritual matters is more transparent; we become more Christ-like in our appearance; we are more forgiving and compassionate to those who have hurt us; and our spiritual perception becomes enlightened as the secret things of God are revealed to us as the inner man is constantly maturing in the Word of God. Spiritual discernment will increase as we learn to listen attentively to the voice of the Holy Spirit. It is important to be spiritually balanced as this will act as a shield to the doctrines of Satan and to the wind of heresies. Additionally, growth will begin to take place in our spiritual life as we are no longer controlled by negative thoughts and influences.

We should never attempt to resolve spiritual hatred with speaking in tongues but with the fruit of the Spirit of God. And likewise, we should always rely on the Holy Spirit to instruct us when counseling others and engaging in spiritual warfare.

When we are called to assist with the needs of others, it should not be done because we are obligated to do so. Instead, it must be done because it is the right thing to do. Often, when we are called to the aid of others, we do not respond with the spirit of Love, but we sometimes respond in the spirit of selfishness and false motives; however with such intentions we are really deceiving ourselves spiritually as well as deceiving those whom we are entrusted to lead.

When we reflect on different cases that we as spiritual leaders have dealt with, we must ask ourselves: "Did we do our deeds in the spirit of Christ-like Love? Did we do our deeds in the spirit of righteousness? Was God's power revealed through the deeds that we have done? What was the motivation behind the deeds that we did to help that individual?" Our answer may be to us a positive one, but the possibility that it may be a resounding negative answer in the Kingdom of God is a testament to our own selfish motives. If the task had been given to us to assist someone in need, then we should do so with gentleness, with Love and with the grace in which the Lord had sent His Son to redeem us from our sin. According to Paul:

> *Is there any such thing as Christians cheering each other up? Do you love me enough to want to help me? Does it mean anything to you that we are brothers in the Lord, sharing the same Spirit? Are your hearts tender and sympathetic at all? Then make me truly happy by loving each other and agreeing wholeheartedly with each other, working together with one heart and mind and purpose. Don't be selfish; don't try to impress others. Be humble, thinking of others as better than yourselves. Don't look out only for your own interests, but take an interest in others, too.*
> —Philippians 2:3-4, NLT

Nevertheless, the good deed that was done for the person in need should never become the catalyst for a good sermon. Some persons who have been helped by others have been spiritually wounded because the help was not offered in the spirit of Love through Christ Jesus. "If it had not been for my help, you would not have been......"

A Christ-like spirit will not reveal to others what gifts were offered to those who are in need. "*But when you give to the needy, ...your giving may be in secret. Then your Father, who sees what is done in secret, will reward you*" (Matthew 6:4, NIV) I spoke to someone once who said "... when I met... they did not have anything. I was the one who helped them... I had to give them food. They did not have anywhere to live; I had to give them shelter."

If God had truly given us the command to help an individual, that individual's personal affairs should not become public knowledge or be the testimony of the giver to the congregation. The unsaved who are listening will never be able to come to the knowledge of God. Therefore, as believers, we should be guided by the Spirit of the Lord, relying on Him for guidance as we carry out our task in helping one another. While we simply will not be able to offer assistance to everyone who asks, our job is to use the gifts and tools that God has equipped us with to win souls for his Kingdom.

This attitude of giving must rather be Christ-centered. If the Lord reveals a word of truth and knowledge, it is for the edifying of the Church.

True discernment is expressed in Love,
but for the gift to be divinely manifested,
one must truly exhibit the fruit of the spirit.

As a minister, I had experienced many personal conflicts in my walk with the Lord. After spending some time seeking the Lord's guidance, he revealed to me that he wanted me to journey to a particular country. I kept what the Lord had revealed to me secret. When I told a minister that I would be traveling, he revealed to me that "The Lord told him that I should not take this journey... because..." The truth was that the minister's 'revelation' was not from the Lord as I was not going anywhere near to where he thought I was planning to go.

The Lord was sending me on a journey where I had never been before. Nevertheless, because I had confided in this minister once before, he was able to falsely instruct me the way he did. Moreover, he was seemingly even speaking under the anointing of the Holy Spirit. If God had not already instructed me, I would have believed this minister. True discernment actually knows the truth, not through fore-knowledge, but through the 'true' revelation of the Holy Ghost as generated from the heart of the Lord. God, who is so rich in Love and in mercy, always prepares His children for the journey ahead.

In order for us to assist those in need, we must learn to remove the beam out of the person's eyes without perverting God's command, without condemning or judging those in need. According to the Pastoral Christian Counseling Association, "We must counsel not to condemn but counsel to offer salvation, restoration and consolation in the word of God."[9] The characteristics of God must be seen in everything that we do in His name.

A true discerning spirit flows from a heart that is not quick to judge or condemn. It is a spirit that walks soberly, consciously and peacefully before God (James 3:17). True spiritual discernment waits on the direction of the Lord. It listens to the voice of God and waits to be prompted by the Holy Spirit. To walk in true discernment expressing the Love of God, the heart needs to be quiet before the Lord and must be in complete reverence and submission wherever we go. God would prefer that we listen quietly and wait patiently on the moving of the Holy Ghost (Isaiah 30:15). The discerner needs the leading of the Holy Spirit to lead, to guide and to reveal the truth, thus enabling the discerner to understand the mind of God. *"Take heed, and be quiet; fear not, neither be fainthearted"* (Isaiah 7:4, KJV). *"It is good that a man should both hope and quietly wait for the salvation of the LORD"* (Lamentations 3:23, KJV).

The word of God is final. Not everyone will agree, but this is the infallible word of God. In light of the different semantic beliefs, here are a few concise notions on true discernment when expressed in Love.

- True discernment is pure and calm.
- True discernment uses the heavenly wisdom of God, grace and the fruit of the Holy Spirit.
- True discernment is rooted in godly insight and pure motives.
- True or genuine spiritual discernment come from a heart of 1 Corinthians 13.
- True discernment comes through a heart that has resolved, relinquished and repented from variance, strife, jealousy and hatred.
- True discernment comes through a heart that is constantly renewing and is driven spiritually in fasting and prayer, and is always seeking and waiting on the direction of the Holy Spirit.
- True discernment comes through a heart that is at peace with God, as well as a heart that has the peace of God in relation to being at peace with others.

---

9 Arno Profile System

- True spiritual discernment comes through a heart that hears and is acquainted with the voice of God.

A heart that is always thoughtful of the mind of God, and not a heart that is always judgmental can be a discerning heart. Our perceived thoughts, our personal purposes and our own selfish dreams will prevent us from hearing the voice of Lord. Therefore, as leaders operating in the different areas or offices of the Church, it is our responsibility to truly evaluate ourselves in the Lord: we should not be selfishly motivated; we should not be too quick to render judgment on others; and the idea of retaliation should not be found among us.

Should a minister so desire to established his own ministry, his motive should be to traverse the highways and byways, seeking those who are lost, by encouraging them to flee from the wrath which is to come, and to seek eternal life for their souls. The idea should be to win souls and bring them into the Kingdom of the Lord, and not to pollute the souls who are already being prepared for the Kingdom. In one particular case, an elder divided a small church of which he was one of the leaders; in doing so, took with him more than half the congregation. This elder was very strategic in pitting some members against the senior leadership of the church. However, he was not able to keep them united because he had reaped where he had not sown, and so the members were left to wander about with no true shepherd to guide them. Some members went to other denominations, while others backslid by going back to the things they had once left behind.

A soul is a precious gem in the Kingdom of the Lord. Therefore, losing one soul to the wiles of the enemy is a serious blow to the laborious work that it takes to win such soul for the Kingdom of God; hence therefore, the Lord will not be pleased. The gift that God has given to each one is specific; He may choose to give more gifts to some than He would give to others, but each gift that He gives is sacred and precious. If God has chosen one to be a deacon, let such person perform his duties within the office of a deacon. The office of a prophet is scarcely available in the churches today, however if one is so anointed by the Lord, he should be allowed to function within his office and he should not be hindered. The gift of the Lord is precious therefore we must understand that He reveals His secrets only to whomever He will.

Not everyone is called to be a pastor, an evangelist, a prayer leader, a prophet or a deacon even though these positions can be some of the most coveted positions in today's churches. Therefore, we should all aim to spiritually assess ourselves as we strive to attain the gifts that we so desire to achieve, so that we can effectively contribute to the edification of the chosen people of God. (It is not about us!) But by doing so, we can be assured that the Church will experience some greater results in the winning of souls, in the healing of the wounded, and in the reviving of those who have strayed.

Jesus declares:

I can do nothing on my own initiative. As I hear, I judge; and my judgment is just, because I do not seek my own will, but the will of Him who sent me.

—John 5:30, NASB

The best time to make any decision or even to discern in Love is when God's voice is activated in me and I am being given directives as what to say. New insight and discernment will come as we listen to the Holy Spirit! The Holy Spirit is Love and so is the source of all gifts through the power of the Holy Spirit...

"I pray that your love may abound still more and more in real knowledge and all discernment."

—Philippians 1:9, NASB

Paul had a revealed revelation from God in relation to his discernment. He realized that true discernment comes from abounding Love, a Love that seeks the best interest of others. A Love that is active and welcoming even to those who are helpless is a Love that is motivated by true commitment and one that enjoys a long-term devotional experience with God. Such Love and devotion are classified as a spiritually healthy relationship with the Lord and with mankind. It is a Love that is self-sacrificing and abounding to all.

In life, there is always an opposite, and so we must all be aware of the deceptive devices of the enemy, of the false discernment that is prevalent among us that is based upon seduction, superstition and fear. Without the

Love of God and without His peace abounding in our hearts, our discernment will be nothing more than suppositional and selfish motivation from an overinflated and evil heart.

The aim of false discernment is to sow seeds of discord, while true Love is based on sowing seeds of Love. Love is transformational. It transcends peace before the discerning of gifts. Such precedes the peace of God that guards the heart from the darts of the enemy. Thus, to sincerely help someone, we must be able to see clearly with Love. This on the other hand, will guard the heart from poisonous arrows.

True discernment is expressed in Love,
but if a person does not repent of his or former deeds,
he or she cannot be fully effective.

Walk Through

Dear Lord,

I know that I have a responsibility to Love, surrender and give my life entirely to You. Oh Lord, I pray that You will help me to listen to Your voice daily and most of all, to apply Your word to my heart before seeing the faults of others.

Lord, I need to know You more. I want my life to be filled with godly insights and motives that are grounded in Love. Consecrate my heart with Your Love so that my ways and attitudes will never be the same again, as I strive to please only You, Lord.

Thank You dear Lord, for answering my prayer, I sense Your presence in my heart as you cleanse and forgive me, which is so renewing. Thank You for granting the serenity of my heart and thank You that I am becoming more mature in Love; help me to discern with good motives through the power of the Holy Spirit.

Help me to understand between spiritual realities and spiritual truth, so that I may avoid the schemes of the enemy, and therefore avoid the dangerous pitfalls of life. Help me to make wise and just decisions in my personal and family life.

In Jesus' name, I pray.

Amen.

Summary And Reflection

Complete the following:

1. _____ sees the outside of the person and or situation and pretends it knows the inside.

2. Godly insight and discernment comes from having _____
_____.

3. Godly motives are rooted in God's _____.

4.   True discernment always:

    a) _____
    b) _____

5. True or False? Love is everything, it comes before peace and peace comes before discernment. _____

6. True or False? Without Love and peace in your heart, your discernment cannot be from the Lord. _____

7. True or False? When the heart is in unrest it can hear from God. _____

EVALUATION AND TEMPERAMENT

Complete the three-part questions:

1. How do you express the spirit of discernment with the spirit of Love in church discipline?

    a) Moderate
    b) With Temperamental Approach
    c) Be Assertive
    d) Prayerfully
    e) Compulsive analytical

2. Explain the above answer.

_____
_____
_____

3. What would be your balance score on the value of True discernment expressed in Love?

    a) Moderate
    b) Sometime
    c) Thoughtful
    d) Thought substitution
    e) Unresponsive

4. Write down some of your goals for ministry along with your expectations.

    _____

    _____

    _____

    _____

5. Write down some of the goals that you desire to accomplish as a result of reading this book.

    _____

    _____

    _____

    _____

6. Write down at least one internal thoughts that you would like to voice. Sandfords points out, "The ability to completely forgive is perhaps the most needful skill requiring restoration in the family today."

    _____

    _____

    _____

    _____

7. Write down some external qualities you admire about yourself, spouse or a friend?

_____

_____

_____

_____

8. When frozen feelings are present in our churches, in our homes and at work, it will adversely affect which areas of life:

    _____

    _____

    _____

9. Write down three things that can cause frozen feelings?

    a) _____

    b) _____

    c) _____

10. Are you having compulsive frozen feelings for anyone? Explain.

    _____

    _____

    _____

LOVE REQUEST

Things that are missing from your life and that you would like to experience; things that will help you be at peace with yourself and most importantly with Jesus in relation to the lesson.

"Search me, O God, and know my heart: try me and know my thoughts…"

—Psalm 139:23, KJV

Write down three words of supplication that you would like to see manifested, reaffirmed and resolved in your life, family and friends.

_____

_____

_____

We must seek to Love and accept each other as we follow the perfect example of Christ.

Love Reveals the Heart of God

If you judge people, you have no time to Love them.

—Mother Teresa

Let the words of my mouth,
and the meditation of my heart,
be acceptable in thy sight, O LORD.

—Psalm 19:14, KJV

CHAPTER THREE

Love Makes our Words Become Acceptable

LOVE IS THE KEYNOTE OF ALL THINGS

Must we emulate the faith of those who lived in the Old Testament era in order to become acceptable unto God? Or, should we offer daily priestly sacrifices required by God? And even so then is this the doorway that leads us from the morass of worldly pleasure, going onward or upward to the high way of righteousness? Is there such a doorway? And, if there is, does this doorway have a name? Yes, we all would imagine, there should be! There surely is. That name is much rather than a description, as it is greater than any other names, titles, and biographies. Such description is found within every keynote to the heart of Almighty God—Love! Love is the description of everything God does.

That personal invitation of the Lord's Love echoes ever so gently to our hearts, an audible voice, with deep peace, His Word: *"Let the words of my mouth, and the meditation of my heart, be acceptable in thy sight, O LORD"* (Psalm 19:14, KJV).

Love is the key to divine truth. It is the most sacrificial gift of all other gifts and by virtue becomes no more the sacrificial Lamb of God, but has become the King of Kings and the Lord of Lords. Such revelatory gift is the only musical strings to God's revelation on which every spiritual blessing in Christ dwells. It is there we experience the most transformational blessings. And, it is here also that we will be transformed from corruption to incorruption as our mind is renewed in the Word of God. This is the most amazing blessings we have in the sight of God. Better yet, apart from salvation, this is the most sacred promise given the human race. That is the

Holy Spirit's indwelling of the Father's Love and the Son's Love. Divine Love, above every merit, is the standard of all other Love relationships. It is the medium through which our worship is acceptable to God.

The Love of Christ is the most noble and acceptable gift before the doorway of God's throne. The greatest affirmation that is given, wherein all can have direct access at the throne of grace; and yet, still obtaining the benefits and the favor of God (Romans 5:2). Love makes our words become acceptable in the sight of God before they are converted into priestly blessings.

Now, through the opened door of grace, we can catch a glimpse of what we will participate in as His children when the Love of Christ is discovered and when we receive the gift of Christ. From its earliest mention, Love as God's gift to the human soul has its price: the price of 'not my will be done, but His will be done in us,' through the acknowledgement of being saved by the grace of the Lord. Upon the revelation of God sending His only begotten Son into the hearts of men, Christ dwelled among us as we beheld His glory (John 1). Thus, God through Christ graciously gave His life for us that we might have eternal life (John 3:16 and Matthew 10:10).

The Bible tells us much about Joshua before He died. He exhorted the children of Israel to the call of self-examination before crossing River Jordan. By drawing their attention to their vows with the Lord's commandment, he described their Love for God. And above all, he emphasized God's purpose for their lives (Joshua 22:5; 23:11). It is as if God, through Joshua, were unveiling a part of himself never before revealed. The Holy Spirit, acting through the leadership of Joshua, did everything he knew was right in keeping the commandments of God. He was faithful. Thus, on the account of his faithfulness, he reminded the children of Israel of the symbolized power, majesty and authority of their deliverance: God's Love.

As Joshua took over from Moses, the first thing he was made aware of with the people of Israel was that only God is real. He is a very present help—a real presence, awesome, majestic, and powerful God. Joshua knew that the covenant requirements were still in place, and thus required obedience and faith. Thus, God gave Joshua the unprecedented privilege of entering into His presence—the Promised Land. You see, Joshua respected the presence of God and the Promised Land of God. Therefore, Joshua understood that Love for God is only expressed through the obedience of God's covenant. Most of us would not remember that, but this is the essence of true covenant relationship, Love—the transformational image of God and the motivation for His creation.

With such requirement, the children of Israel's relationship with God were to define the principles of 'complete obedience and complete loyalty.' This was the command on which their continued formula of worship through the book of Joshua would be revealed.

The recurring theme of the Bible is focused on Love and covenant obedience. In every case, Love is not an option. In fact, it is the demonstrated proof of the image of God living within us. For that reason, Love is a command with an action of commitment. It is not just feelings but transformational feelings. One of such qualifications is the validation of miracles in the midst of ministry. Is this not what truly makes one a child of God? Is a child of God one who is loved-filled, faith-filled, hope-filled, and unhesitant? Could a child of God be a hungry soul who feeds not just his/her own but feeds others, inspired by the examples of Jesus and the conviction of faith, hope and love? Yes, this is the true mark of discipleship.

We know the first greatest commandment is to Love the Lord with all our heart. And the second greatest commandment is to Love our neighbor as ourselves (Luke 10:27). As Christians, we must make decisive and personal choices to serve God (Deuteronomy 5:6; 11:13) by walking in His ways and fearing His commandments (Deuteronomy 8:6b). God deserves the truth, surrounded by relationship, responsibility and resolution; out of the womb of repentance and reconciliation without representation, to support our request being flawless and acceptable in His sight. It is my strongest belief that God is calling the church out of the womb of repentance, reconciliation and recompilation without representation, as His bride to impact the world with His revival power—Love. As out of the womb of repentance, revival is birth. That is what the Lord wants for His church.

We must be careful with the choice of words we use when preaching, counseling or even having a conversation. The contents of words are very important—words are the document that affirmed life, ignited liberty, and compelled us to pursue happiness with Love to our God and our family.[10]

---

10 Samuel Rodriguez, "The Lamb's Agenda," (Dallas, Thomas Nelson Publisher, 2013), pg. 195.

Joshua's entire focus was on the monument of God's Word, as compared to his past leadership with Moses (Joshua 1: 5-17). With a strong force of the Love of the Lord, the children of Israel in the wilderness were kept alive, and favorably given the Promised Land—this was a gift from God. This pious leader demonstrated to all that one can muster confidence despite doubt and perhaps even because of it (see Joshua 1). Sometimes when things are going our way, we tend to forget the benefits of God's Love (see Psalm 103). These Israelites were no different. They witnessed faith, hope and Love as they wrestled with unbelief. But through the hidden typology of grace—the Love of Christ—God's death sentence upon the children of Israel was canceled because God's Son spoke peace to the heart of His Father, which prevented the execution of the children of Israel in the wilderness.

God had told Moses to speak to the rock, but he did otherwise. That rock is Jesus, the all sufficient One, embodied as the Rod of Aaron, the Cleft of the Rock, and the Pillar of cloud by day and the Pillar of fire by night. Praise the Lord, by the grace of Jesus' Love, we are greatly blessed and highly favored children of God, though we are imperfect we are forgiven children of God.

Moses had to be reminded of God's commands pulling at him. Moses disqualified himself from being faith, hope and Love and more accurately fell under the category of disobedience, even though he was the meekest man who ever lived. True love welcomes suggestions and questions; false love discourages and prohibits them. Nevertheless, let us not forget that if all the questions are answered, we would have satisfied ourselves too easily. On this earth, we will never know God in all His glory—we cannot. Faith thus remains the assurance of grace hoped for and the conviction of better things to come; while Love teaches that faith and hope can walk together, casting out perfect fear and thus by conquering all. An example of the children's relationships with God would be a reflection of their worship, as love by marriage declares, "*cleave unto the Lord your God, as ye have done unto you this day*" (Joshua 23:8, KJV). "*Keep yourselves in the Love of God, looking for the mercy of our Lord Jesus Christ unto eternal life*" (Jude 1:21, KJV).

Joshua in particular, admonished the greatest commandment of God referred in Luke 10:27,

Thou shalt love the Lord thy God with all thy heart, and with all thy soul, and with all thy strength, and with all thy mind; and thy neighbor as thyself.

—Luke 10:27, KJV

By nature, Joshua understood the deceit of the heart in response to the condition of pleasure and to the profession of truth. And so, the concept of Joshua's last sermon to the children of Israel was to implant in their hearts the Love and admonition of God. These were practically identical and often repeated as command conditions, demonstrated in both testaments as the standards of God for holy living. Far above everything else, the allegiance of the people's hearts was to always respond in Love to God's sovereignty. As they responded in their Love to God, their lives would be extended, and their gifts would be accepted as promised (Psalm 40:6; 1 Samuel 15:22). Although Love cannot be seen, it affects everything we do. When Joshua sent the Reubenites, Gadites, and half-tribe of Manasseh back to their homes by the eastern side of the Jordan, he admonished them to take heed to do the commandment and Law of Moses. The children of Israel gladly served the Lord with all their hearts being motivated by God's promised Love. In fact, they served without seeing God, but through the likes of Moses' and Joshua's teachings, their confidence in God was magnified.

And now, O Israel, what does the LORD your God ask of you but to fear the LORD your God, to walk in all his ways, to love him, to serve the LORD your God with all your heart and with all your soul...

—Deuteronomy 10:12, NIV

The object of our worship should not shift from God to mammon (see Matthew 6:24). The throne of Jesus is much more important than any other throne, and the ways of pleasing God should not change from loving and fearing Him. This strategy used by Joshua was the means by which God would reveal His character to the children of Israel. Any than that done with Love, with word and with good deed would not be delighting or become acceptable unto God (Jeremiah 9: 23–24).

You see, Loving God is seeking His ways. With our genuine faithfulness to please Him in all things, we push out our little bud of faith from its branches. This way, we are filled with a sense of promise and hope. And, it is this sense of promise and hope that is conveyed by the rainbow of His presence on our first green leaves that may signify the awesome power and glory of God's character in us. His immutability and the steadfastness of His Word are glorious! What God says He will do, He will do. Similarly, the same way we expected our spouses and our children to please us, the Lord expects us to please Him (Job 22:21). Difficult circumstances can turn around for us if we are committed to make a difference in our relationships. Joshua and the rest of Bible leaders used this very important approach with the children of Israel, as:

> *This book of the law shall not depart out of thy mouth, but thou shalt meditate therein day and night, that thou mayest observe to do according to all that is written therein: for then thou shalt make thy way prosperous, and then thou shalt have good success.*
> —Joshua 1: 8, ERV

> *When all Israel has come to appear before the Lord your God at the place which he shall choose, you shall read this law before all Israel in their hearing.*
> —Deuteronomy 31:11, ESV

> *And the king went up into the house of the LORD, and all the men of Judah and all the inhabitants of Jerusalem with him, and the priests, and the prophets, and all the people, both small and great: and he read in their ears all the words of the book of the covenant which was found in the house of the LORD.*
> —2 Kings 23:2, KJV

> *Day after day, from the first day to the last, Ezra read from the Book of the Law of God. They celebrated the feast for seven days, and on the eighth day, in accordance with the regulation, there was an assembly.*
> —Nehemiah 8:18, NIV

Love is a catalyst like the process of photosynthesis in plant transformation. Energy from the sun converts the substance within the plants from which the manufacturing of food is produced. As sunlight is necessary for the process of photosynthesis, likewise is wisdom for spiritual development. Both changes are of paramount importance within the lives of the plant and the total man. Regarding such process in relation to our spiritual walk, we should desire the gift of Love and the gift of wisdom in order to lead others successfully.

Not only was Joshua guided by the word of God but he also observed and did the will of God too. It is much easier to set goals when we have received guidance and Love from the Holy Spirit, and especially from a discerning spiritual mentor. Moses prepared a leader who would take God's people farther than he ever could. This is what good leaders do. Sometimes people failed in God's exams as a result of the lack of Love, obedience and devotion to God. If we have the command, but we do not know what they say, of course we will fail. The same is said of God's word; we could meditate and study day and night, but if we do not have Love, we will fail miserably. Thus, the bottom line is, we will become a sounding brass and our works will not be acceptable to God. Likewise, when we reject God's way, sooner or later the result will be failure, fear and frustration.

If we truly want success in life, we must serve God by meditating upon His Word, loving others and be faithful to our families. It is much easier when we have someone wiser and successful to help us. Just as God promised to be with Joshua in his meditation and physical battles, so He promised to be with us in our spiritual walk.

God often times compares our Love for Him to that of a lover (see Ephesians 6). It is interesting to look back into the Old Testament and to see how these same figures were used in the marching order of holy matrimony. It is much easier as well to see the characteristics represented here—patience, endurance, faithfulness and perseverance. Man has the intelligence, personality and the spiritual/emotional makeup of God within him. We now have the whole scene before us. In the center is the throne of Almighty God in all its glory; He gives us His descriptions of the nature of a loving relationship. By God's standard of such relationships, He expects us to follow the pattern of His perspective for doing His will. Similarly, we desire to accomplish intimate communion with our spouse, and God expects the same.

Every word that we exchange is precious in God's sight (Isaiah 43:4). This is one of the most reassuring comments that label our relationship and is pleasing to the Lord. We find that this shows the truth of God's Love as well. The word of God goes on to say that we are dear to His heart, which is one of the many reasons He has been defending us from the snares of the enemy.

In a miraculous way, with His precious Love, He bestowed His favor on us. Therefore, we are precious in the sight of God. Thus, we should promote the welfare of His church beyond the call of duty. For more than the call of duty, we are to defend His Love where the companies of hatred have been campaigning. And above all, we are to proclaim the truth of His Love in time of calamity.

Our outmost confidence should be to raise the empire of Christ's Love, by converting our neighborhoods, transforming surrounding communities, and by enunciating the richness of God's Love to impact lives with the names of Jesus. We are all called to serve, but are we accomplishing the task to which we have been called? Is it known that the calling of the Lord on our lives into ministry is to serve people? That is ministry and that is the mission and purpose of the Church—the marketplace! Thus, being called to serve is the duty of Loving through leading and leading by Loving. As we do this, we will preserve the foundation of our next generation.

Christ's mission cost Him His life as He protected our lives from the wiles of Satan. Christ emerged from death as the first fruit of God's Love (1 Corinthians 15:20). The investments and freedom in God's Love of those who have passed on are precious and honorably well done. In other words, these saints are now comfortably and gently relieved from earthly rest to the heavenly best in God. This emphasizes our service in God's Love comparing to earthly recognition.

> *Since you were precious in my sight, you have been honorable, and I have loved you: therefore will I give men for you, and people for your life.*
>
> —Isaiah 43: 4, AKJV

In Isaiah's view, we have been distinguished differently from the public face of the world. Hidden from the public face of grace, the fear of life was beefed up with the fear of Mosaic Law and death. But God in relation to Christ's Love assures Love to everyone (see John 3:16). In history, God offered a more profitable Love under grace than the old era of the law. God's perfect Love was a theocratic Love which is above all other worldly Loves. This Love is greater than feelings, and is fruitful love. And for that reason, God's love not only concerns spiritual matters but is also the transformational power of Christ in us, which gives us the hope of being resurrected. Within such love comes its assignment, which is to impact the word in like manner with Christ's assignment when He was on earth. Perfect love in Christ not only casts out all fears but overcomes evil with good.

In short, God's birthright is Love. This is why His health care program for the believer is Love which is the best wealth for soul health. In referring to Himself in this context, Jesus declared to John, the beloved of Christ, *"Beloved, I wish above all things that thou mayest prosper and be in health, even as thy soul prospereth"* (3 John 1:2, KJV). That is the true source of Love—to accomplish a divine mandate of charity and instructive provision of the soul. It is very important that we achieve this Love and also understand the vastness of God's Love.

Despite the different convictions of faith, Christ's Love is the empirical foundation on which the promises of eternal life stand. Ultimately, this is the acceptable entrance to Heaven—the key to God's heart, Love!

The campaigning motive of the devil is to engineer skepticism into our hearts. He does this because he is an opportunist. We know that he is waiting for the perfect opportunity to launch his own politics into our hearts. But we are not ignorant of his devices! Much more important than the devil's invention is the personality of his plans. Many of his plans always come to naught against the counsel of the Love of God. None can in any way compare with the throne on which sits the triune God—the Father, the Son, and the Holy Spirit. First, this throne is significantly rebuilt and reinforced with heavenly colors. The best sets of roles are ever there (Love, peace, joy, etc.).

Much disaster will happen, but God will keep His covenant and will not allow the enemy to destroy it completely. Thus, the tea party of Satan's regime will never prevail against the beauty of God's sunset, the glory of God's sunrise and the glory of His eternal power. One may have thought the devil would give up when we are serving God but he never does. This is the reason we have to stay submerged in the Word of God, and as well as to keep afloat on the wings of His Love. Do you know that the devil is persistent? Yes, but God is in control, regardless. Yet in the midst of all this, we see Satan reveal another aspect of his character here. Not as an angel of light but as a counterfeiting spirit by which he duplicates an environment that is reproduced by legalism, and hence reveals hatred and chaos. There is something else we can learn here, too. In the first *pericope* or section of Galatians 5, the Bible refers to these as strongholds. Such demonic strongholds appear to be jealousy, variance, lasciviousness, incest, killing, sorcery, drunkenness, carousing, immorality and licentiousness (see Galatians 5).

I am sure that the devil's schemes will never last. This is another indication that Love is not a nebulous feeling but is substantial, transformational and real, just as God is substantial, is transformational and is real. Jesus wants us to know also that He is the way, the truth and the life. Jesus and God care deeply for everyone, and feel compassion for us. Thus, they are one in heart, Love, deity, church administration and family administration. Despite the different social issues we face in life, through this we are deeply Loved by God.

Jesus is a warm and caring spirit. We are to show Love despite the erroneous teachings of other religions. In the sight of God's Love, we are to prevent hatred in our hearts at the disposal of God's holiness. We are precious in the sight of God and Christ. Here, we have been chosen as God's blessed family with all spiritual blessings with the eyes of Love, above principalities and power. And there, we were desired and betrothed for eternity as Jesus undertook death. With God's help, Jesus implanted His treasures in us, comparing us to precious stones. To be sure, Christ Jesus calls us pearls of great price. We are precious and most honorable in the esteem of God's and Christ's Love.

The nature of our relationship with others can only appear before God when the Love of Christ by birth, by regeneration, and by righteousness is favored with the presence of God and Christ. Only when our life is purchased with Christ's Love and blood can our souls be redeemed with God in eternity. Love is an act in eternity and His blood is the redeeming path to eternity. The word of God teaches that in time past we were nothing but grace sought us. This is an inspired past act, upon the revelation of Jesus as Christ and the Son of the living God. Thus, this is also an act in eternity where God delighted and continued in Love to make us precious and honorable. On such note, God rested in His Love as an act of unmerited grace. Today God's Love is laid out and uniquely waiting to transform us from mortality to immortality, and from grace to glory.

Christ's Love is the source and spring of all other Love qualities. As I mentioned earlier, it is unchangeably the same; it never alters its characterization. Our actions should be fully motivated at the expense of our words of appreciation, in an effort to prove our Love, our commitment to God and to our family. Today, more than ever, we need a spirit of Pentecost which will enable us to speak the heavenly language, not in the spirit of political correctness, but rather in the spirit of biblical correctness. In like manner with God, in order to please Him in all things, the Lord wants us to practice the lesson taught in Joshua *"Be very careful, therefore, to love the LORD your God"* (Joshua 23:11, ESV).

This is the same message throughout the Bible: Love. By contrast, the Lord wants us to live according to His commandments. As promised, He will greatly bless those who do His perfect will. Thus, those who disobey the commandments of God will find greater setback attached to everything they do. Regardless of our good deeds and works, the Lord will never be pleased with us if our immediate Love amplifies other gods. The notion of our Love will then not become acceptable to God. This is because Love is the keynote that reveals the secret of the human heart.

The home on the other hand should be a haven of Love. Honor, courtesy and respect symbolize Love and characterize the righteous family.

In one of Job's conversations with God and possibly with his friends, he asked one of the most resounding, authentic, and heartfelt questions: How forcible are words? (Job 6:25) As unconventional as Job was, this was a time of heart searching for him. Job perhaps believed God did not understand what he was going through. In spite of personal failures that denied him any meaningful recovery, the Lord made sure that Job was prepared for restoration. We all, at some point, come to the end of the road like Job did.

Job's health and wealth along with his family were restored. Can you imagine that a day did not go by when Job did not continue to grieve for the loss of his first seven children? The pain did not magically just go away. The grief was real, but through the presence of God's Love, one day at a time, through a life of intense prayer, Job experienced the grace of God's Love. We too, have discovered this in our struggles. But with Christ Jesus, we can get through the pain. Many people have been impacted by grave situations and uncomfortable challenges may seem unbearable. It may even seem as if it is not going to end. Nevertheless, struggles and problems do not last forever, they have their expiration date. In fact, they put us in a place of destiny and purpose, and thus stir us up.

I believe words have the power to repair a broken heart and make dreams come true. They have the power to enforce their desires and make the person feels better about themselves. And they also have the power to inflict wounds to the broken hearted, and to keep dreams from coming to reality. Words also have the power to tear us down and make us feel completely unwanted. This is the fundamental reason we are to always strive to keep hatred from babbling into our hearts and out of our minds.

When hatred is within us, it is a guarantee that nothing good will come from it. The Bible teaches that *"out of the abundance of the heart his mouth speaks"* (Luke 6:45, ESV). Words are the voice of the heart and above all the harmony of the heart. When our words are consistently demeaning, undermining, critical, unkind—negative emotions will dominate our hearts. Before we realize it, our words then will become unacceptable to God. And so God cannot bless us, our homes or our children when our hearts are infiltrated with darkness. As noted from many past experiences, this will most definitely breed contention in any relationships. And this will furthermore create unnecessary questions, and thus later filter the spirit of unfaithfulness.

Where Love is, there is no disputing. Where Love resides, there is no contention. Where Love is, there God will be. Each one of us has the responsibility to keep God's commandments. Yes, this is wisdom embedded in the Scriptures to challenge us at every stage of life.

In this world, there is a tendency for us to need change, to require help, and to desire relief. But with the desire to serve God, we fail to define Love, and therefore we must do something about it. How can we Love God when there is no peace in our hearts? Will our gifts be accepted? (See Psalm 66:18; 18:23.) Love is the first and greatest commandment of God. It does not grow like a weed or fall like rain. It is given as well as received through the gifts of surrendering to God's Love.

A heart of Love is a heart of Jesus. A heart of Jesus is a heart of helping. And a heart of helping is getting the job done. *"Inasmuch as ye have done it unto one of the least of these my brethren, ye have done it unto me"* (Matthew 25:40, KJV). I extend my sincere regard to those who with loving care and compassionate concerns feed the hungry, clothe the naked and house the homeless. He who notes the sparrow's fall will be mindful of such service.[11]

---

11   Thomas S. Monson, https://www.lds.org/general-conference/1987/10/a-doorway-called-Love?

That said, in His messianic ministry Jesus administered Love to a deceased family by resurrecting him to life. He offered the ministry of compassion with these words:

> *When the Lord saw her, His heart went out to her and He said, "Don't cry," then he went up and touched the bier....and said: "Young man, I say to you, get up."*
>
> —Luke 7: 11–15, NIV

The word of God teaches Love conquers all. In Love and compassion, Jesus raised the dead. Our Love in Christ has the motivating power to combat death sentences over our families. We can thus command things to happen through the spiritual realm.

The desire to uplift, the willingness to help, and the graciousness to give come from a heart filled with Love. Love is the noblest attribute of the human soul that symbolizes complete care and concern for others.

As Christians, our philosophy should decisively be doing our best to share the Love of Christ. Our responsibilities should not fail with broken promises. Jesus showed us His Love by dying on the cross. After He died, He rose triumphantly from the grave and took the keys of death and hell, and thus gave us the most amazing miracle—the gift of the Holy Spirit. That is the Father's Love! As we have been affectionately accepted through Jesus' blood, we are to show His Love by helping those in need.

True Love is a reflection of Christ's Love. The moment we stop showing that Love is the moment we will lose our humanity; that is the moment we deny Christ and that is the moment we become unfaithful. We cannot afford to lose our future by disregarding others. As Jesus battled with the agony of Gethsemane and the excruciating pain on the cross, tears gushed down His mother's face. The affection of Love cried out in Jesus and He gave His mother into the keeping of His beloved disciple (John 19: 26–27). Love will endure and will echo the spirit of forgiveness even when the doorway of Jesus' heart is impacted. Through this, the wondrous gift is given and the blessings of heaven were received. On the promise side, the Lord imparts His Love, His will, and His life.

But after Mary experienced the bestowed Love of Jesus on resurrection morning, her joy was fulfilled. There, Mary realized that the greatest affirmation above everything and beyond anything that this world has to offered is God's Love (John 15:13). Our ticket to Heaven is guaranteed as promised by Jesus (Ephesians 1:13; John 14). Will you not Love Him? Will you not serve Him? By loving and serving Christ, we are forwarding our application to heaven, as a means to assure a crown in Christ's heart (1 John 4:6).

You see, where there is Love, there be no record of disputing. A happy contented person who truly appreciates others by loving, by forgiving and by blessing their spouse and others, does not have the time to transfer hatred.

Kind words can be short and easy to speak,
but their echoes are truly endless.
—Josh Billings

Demonstrating Love with kind words is more than talk. It is rather a heart experience, with greater impulsive desires that geminates its seeds within an environment full of affection. Likewise, it participates best when its qualities are met through:

- Edifying (to build up, uplift each other, secular or spiritual, Ephesians 4:29)

- Encouraging (to give support, to inspire with hope to do something or to pour out into; Deuteronomy 3:28; Isaiah 41:10, Joshua 3:9, Numbers 13:30)

- Esteeming others (to regard highly with respect, to consider as of a certain value, to appraise, favorable opinion or judgment, express true appreciation. Philippians 2: 3, Romans 12:10; Galatians 5:26, 1 Peter 3:8)

- Giving blessing and praise (to God and others for work being done through faithfulness and favor. Psalm 9:1, 2; 34: Hebrews 13:15; Numbers 6:24–26)

- Being without evil and malice (Psalm 34:13, Ephesians 4:31)

- Showing kindness (Ephesians 5:20, 1 Thessalonians 5:18)

- Being truthful and honest (Proverbs 12:19, 22; Ephesians 4:15; Colossian 3:9)

- Being without gossip (Psalm 15:1, 3; Proverbs 11:13)

- Being genuine and pure (Proverbs 15: 4, 26, Ephesians 4:29).

Along with the soul, Love satisfies the heart with the tranquility of Christ's fragrance. The Love of Christ beautifies our hearts with the estate of His delight. There is nothing in God's Love that can cause loathing; no infinity or deformity can quench His Love for us. There is nothing Love produces that is below standard. As well, there is that mystic excellence in Love which may not only invite our souls to God, but also command our souls to worship in spirit and truth (John 4:24). Only Love could cause Christ to die for sinners.

Worldly things will die and leave us but the Love of God is forever, (Hebrews 13:8). Absolutely, there is no danger in loving God. He is the comforter in our nights, a refuge for the broken hearted and a lighthouse to the blind (John 1:4). It is better to Love the Lord; surely it is better to Love the Lord than this world (1 John 4:5-7) as the Lord will quickly forgive us, but the world will not. Instead, the world will hate and despitefully use us (Matthew 5:11–12). You see, the world is beautiful, but how much comfort does the world give? It is like the weeds that wrap our hearts with desire for pleasures and successes. But does the world inspire us to Love and forgive our neighbor? It perhaps will, but temporarily with frozen Love. By contrast, the Love of the Lord is like a running stream. For without this Love, the Lamb's agenda could not be fulfilled. There is no frozen ice too hard that His Love cannot melt.

Some plants will not thrive when they are closely planted together. The Love of God will allow us to thrive and grow freely together (See John 15). This is because the flower of Love produces a greater effervescence that transcends with the peace of unity. Such Love weakens, corrodes and destroys the Spirit of disunity, declaring *"that your love may abound more and more in real knowledge and all discernment…filled with the fruit of righteousness…"* (Philippians 1:9-11, NASB). Love is a pure flame kindled from heaven, which God uses to create us into His perfect image. This is the reason the psalmist could say: "*For we are fearfully and wonderfully made*" (Psalm 139:14, NIV). Without Love our religion would be in vain.

It is only when we partake of Christ's Love that we become acceptable to God (John 15:10–13). Being born again is the greatest experience one could ever have, receiving the life of Christ (John 15:11–16). In this experience, our spirit is joined with Christ, wherein Jesus' identification with us is completed. As a result of this, our lives are no longer the object of the first Adam but are the culmination of Christ's resurrected Love; by which His Love is immensely burning in us, forever changing the way we see others. God is the most infinite and complete object of our Love; through His death, He bore our sins and suffered. And in His resurrection, He became our life, so much that in His spirit we are even joined with Him.

The fragrance of Christ is Love. He is filled with the fragrance of His nature. And He is the essence of His nature, Love. According to Paul:

Now thanks be to God who always leads us in triumph in Christ, and manifests through us the sweet aroma of the knowledge of him in every place. For we are a fragrance of Christ to God among those who are being saved and among those who are perishing.
—2 Corinthians 2:24–15

This great revelation of Jesus Christ gives us an inner assurance that whenever the Father looks upon us, He therefore sees only the righteousness and the cheerful Love of Jesus Christ's aromatherapy imbedded in us. Thus, we are accepted by these precious promises declared two thousand years ago, and as stated in 2 Corinthians 1:20–22, "...*all the promises of God are yes and amen, to the glory of God through us...He who establishes ...*" (1 Corinthians 1:20–22, NKJV). Have we been born again? Yes! Praise the Lord; we have also been filled with His spirit! By being accepted as a peculiar person, this further gives us hope, in that our lives take on a new meaning in Christ. This way, we all can enter into the Spirit of God's presence, with the assurance that our gifts are being accepted. According to the Apostle Paul, "...*by whom also we have access by faith into this Grace wherein we stand, and rejoice in hope of the glory of God*" (Romans 5:2, KJV).

It is not just words from our mouth that can last a long time. Instead, our life itself can, through the acceptance of either Christ or Satan. Who would have thought this has the power to last forever (John 3:15)? But, this is the act of choice which determines our eternal bliss or eternal damnation. Are our hearts centered on sin or have our hearts discovered Love? Without the heart being transformed, the heart of the Lord's theocracy will never take us beyond the pearly gate of heaven. What difference does it make, beyond our own personal relationship with God, if we begin with Love? The relationship we have entered into and stand in with God is Love. That is the difference! You see, Love is the only maker of husbandry that is filled with tenderness and rejoices with the spouse. It is as the bridegroom awaits her bride, so is the grace of Love. She prepares herself as the bride to meet the bridegroom. Many have become the apple of God's eyes, as His bride of Love in anticipation with the coming of the Lord, as portrayed by the Word of God in Matthew 25.

We are His precious treasures that have been protected from the pirates of sin in order to meet our Maker (Amos 4). According to God's assurance:

> *For this is what the Lord Almighty says: "After the Glorious One has sent me against the nations that have plundered you—for whoever touches you touches the apple of his eye…"*
> —Zechariah 2:8, NIV

Love is the only gift that will divinely position and thus appoint us into Heaven (John 15:16; Ephesians 2:6–7). While the remaining gifts will only take us to the doorway of faith and hope, Love will continue and thus goes beyond faith and hope (1 Corinthians 13) and there present us into the pearly gate of heaven. On this ground of affirmation, we can be assured that being called to Love and serve our neighbors in Christ will not be in vain. As the power of Love heals the nation, Love also passionately satisfies the hearts with the treasures of heaven, as we abide in Him (John 15:1–11).

Every human being needs Love. With Love, we grow and delight in each other. For example, Jacob's Love for Rachel was unconditional and like Christ in that Jacob faithfully sacrificed another seven years of committed labor prior marrying Rachel. Their Love for each other was exceptionally divine and beyond human infatuation. Every opportunity they had was a ministry unto the Lord, as Jacob and Rachel sought for ways of improvement, to maintain their faithfulness and honesty in Love. Thus, their trust in each other only fueled their patience unto an immense flame of Love that kept their relationship burning, as hope fuels faith. Despite waiting for fourteen years, they never lost hope of their Love. Although many situations arose where Jacob and Rachel could have deserted each other, God's divine assignment for their lives was preordained and thus unfolded to be bigger than their personal vision. When we look at their testimonial faith and setbacks, it is worth mentioning to admonish younger couples, as it relates to courtship, to listen to wisdom while waiting and even listen to hear God's voice before saying 'yes, I will marry you.'

We should endeavor always to lean on the Lord for His perfect counseling and heavenly wisdom. This is absolutely necessary as Love makes waiting a pleasure by oiling the wheel of patience with grace. That way, our requests presented to God, both as a living and as a holy sacrifice are cheerful. Love is not impatient as many have conceived, even though it may come with longsuffering. Otherwise, he that Loves God is never weary of telling it. And he that Loves His family is never too busy to show it.

Love is the expression of showing and serving God, family and others. Both bring out the same expression and the best expression harmoniously. Dr. Stephen Covey believes we all have an 'Emotional Bank Account,' that is only active or alive when daily deposits and withdrawals of Love, of faithfulness and of trust are being made.[12] He believes this is the means on which the account is maintained. And so, I believe the same can be said about our spiritual life in regard to repentance.

The water of repentance is not pure unless it flows from the spring of genuine Love. This is true and in fact is parallel to a lasting and effective relationship with Jesus Christ and more frankly with our spouse. As where there is no Love, hatred and jealousy will increase. Love shows support and by doing that wins the lost at any cost.

By loving Christ, we automatically grow and become more like Him. Unless Love flows from within a heart of submission, our works are not acceptable to God (1 Peter 3:7). Repentance is the only source to God's wrought revival. It is always the principles and not the methods that are righteousness and justice. Other than that, the cry of man's heart of being restored unto God's first love is rootless and is fruitless. Through such

---

12 Patrick Morley, Seven Seasons of the Man in the Mirror (Grand Rapids: Michigan, 1995), 112.

requirement, the doors of revival will never close. Thus, it is the only GPA system (G:God, P:Power and A:Analysis) that can originally take us back to the solace of God's throne, as well as reconciling our first love with His heart of Love. There is therefore no other structural blueprint given or outline to be reconciled unto the Lord, except that man must be born again through the blood of Jesus, by the Spirit of Jesus and by the Word of Jesus.

> *Likewise, ye husbands, dwell with them according to knowledge, giving honour unto the wife, as unto the weaker vessel, and as being heirs together of the grace of life; that your prayers be not hindered.*
> —1Peter 3:7, KJV

> *Jesus answered, "Very truly I tell you, no one can enter the Kingdom of God unless they are born of water and the Spirit."*
> —John 3:5, NIV

In like manner also, the same can be said of our relationships with our spouses. In particular, unless there are frequent deposits of Love, communication and trust into our 'Emotional Bank Account' the flow of Love will become lukewarm. The amount of Love that we normally withdraw from our account will one day become empty. In fact, this is the most accurate concept to build on. The aim of this policy will never give a lower Love exchange rate, but rather seeks the best interest rate of its own. Nevertheless, whenever there is a tremendous overdraft, the experience can be very embarrassing, depressing and deserting to anyone.

Today, many have discovered and are enjoying this concept; while on the other hand, others are experiencing serious problems as a result of mismanagement. And since, this is paralleled to relationships today, it is necessary that immediate steps be taken to resolve these issues in the family. This reality is real and does happen. Therefore, it is worth encouraging lasting and effective relationships, so that our children can emulate these family traits for the next generation.

It is definitely necessary that our Love tank should always carry an estimation of value. This way, the flow of Love within the relationship will not breed unhealthy questions that are demeaning and are not edifying. Nevertheless, it should be noted that, sometimes it is quite possible to drive on a half tank, but it is not recommended to drive on empty since this can be dangerous and thus can compound the matter even more.

As we grow, by taking on additional responsibilities, it is our duty to maintain our relationships with Christ and with our spouses. When our Love tank is filled with genuine Love, honest deposits and faithful withdrawals are evident. Such attributes ignite more trust and Love. Likewise, spending time together will also be more meaningful. And of course, a greater desire of helping each other will delete misunderstanding, frustration, assertive authority and other dysfunctional behaviors. With a stronger sense of humility and synergy, both partners will have a better season of communication and a stronger covenant of love, thus avoiding running on low or empty, a kind of love bankruptcy. Love bankruptcy is a spiritual disease caused by excuses, such as lying and lasciviousness which it is then filtered into mismanagement of love, fun times, attention, and service, as well as improper care of communication, administration, trust and understanding. Such are the characteristics of incompatible relationships and incompatible leadership. Such people take pleasure in constantly doing the same things over and over again without showing any remorse in their actions.

The wise and conscientious couple would have their Love account examined in view of their relationship unto God, and by demonstrating the meaning of loving each other. Their complimentary lives will always have extra fuel to rely on. This is similar to the wise man who built his house on a rock, and likewise to the foolish man that built his house on sandy shore. We are told that the storm destroyed the house on the sandy ground, but the house on the solid rock was not affected by the storm. When our Love tank is dried or empty, the tendency for separation and divorce normally creeps in. Therefore, what we feel internally should never be taken lightly, as this can have a lasting effect on the way we respond emotionally, socially, mentally and even spiritually to family and friends. Most of the time, the individual usually nurses, nurtures, rehearses and secures the feelings emotionally, without connecting his feelings to others. Thus, we should be encouraged and praise God for delivering us from such perilous sin. There is no doubt that God is with us, therefore with confidence let us raise our Love and be inspired to make daily deposits into our Love account.

The Love of God is the most abiding grace. Even when our Love tank is empty, the Love of God will refuel our vessels, and gladly stay with us. When faith, hope and grace are gone, Love continues. The job of Love is to prevent sin from entering our hearts, thus making it possible for us to present our gifts before the throne of heaven. How can we be accepted in the Kingdom of God? There is only one way, and that is by loving, serving and obeying God.

As you know, everything we do in life is either a deposit or a withdrawal of something. God desires us to continue to make these transactions as a means to balance our different account of life (See 1 Corinthians 2:9).

The Word of God says we are to Love our wives so that our prayers can be answered (1 Peter 3:7). As we Love with words, we are agreeing with the will of God. Thus, the greatest benefits are given to us when we Love God against all errors, wind of doctrines and delusions. If we Love God, we have the wind of God blowing our way; everything will work for our good.

Now is the time to Love without assimilation. Now is the time to forget the injustice and cultivate the spirit of Love. It is your life that has been affected and has experienced brokenness. God is saying, 'Love me and I will teach you to Love others without the struggles of unforgiving.' He reminds us that 'this is the way to my true identity. This is the way to my Love, because I am the way, the truth, and the life to Love you with measureless purpose.'

Love is like watering the tree to make it grow. For example, as in the parable of the seed in Matthew 13, many lives have fallen apart because their roots never survived, but the Lord's love was still immutable. You may have been trampled on the ground and words may have been spoken over your life, or perhaps those seeds that were sown never grew or germinated as you had expected. Nevertheless, the Lord's blessings are sure as His promise concerning the plan and purpose He has ordained for us are yes and amen.

The Lord has given us great consolation, through which we can declare His promises over our lives, by advancing His kingdom and thus by enlarging our territory like Jabez. The word of God says, "He who Loves God will cleave to Him," as Ruth clung to Naomi, and Joshua to God. (See Genesis 2:24 and Ephesians 5:25.) He who wants to Love the Lord will not do as Orpah did to her mother-in-law by insinuating her privilege. It is our choice that leads to blessing or cursing, and so, there is a pathway that leads to eternal life and also a pathway that leads to damnation. Our choices, like Orpah's, can determine our destiny. However, God is in charge because He oversees the future of this world. With God Loving us, we must Love Him too. But there can be no successful relationship with God other than falling in Love with Him over and over again.

We have a tendency to grow more in Love with the world, as opposed to growing more in Love with Christ and with others. But in all cases, the latter is always greater and is better than the former, as it will help us to Love faithfully. This is attributed to the uniqueness of God's image molding us like the clay in the potter's hands.

When Jesus was in the Garden of Gethsemane praying, and also on the Cross, His Father forsook Him twice. Being in pain and agony, Jesus' lamented according Psalm 22 and Matthew 27. At this crucial point of justification, there was nothing God could do, because Jesus was already clothed with the garment of our sin. He chose to take this upon Himself. By human nature, we would despise Jesus' suffering and God's condemnation and separation from Jesus. But God is not open to our different perceptions. We may even have more question than answers. Of course, this is perfectly right, but we remember that the word of God comes from the mind of God and therefore the Lord's order does not change with the ambition of God. If this was the case, the whole earth, both heaven and earth would have been infected with the virus of pride, which was developed in hatred and jealousy. Thus, as a result, God had to stop Satan from spreading pride to His Son and the rest of the angels in heaven.

In heaven, God had to take action. God cannot see or look upon sin; He only can see the blood of Jesus. By this principle, therefore, He could not rescue Jesus because Jesus had taken on the nature of the world, which is the nature of sin. As you know, light and darkness are two opposites, just as law and grace, and salvation and sin. They are neither synonymous nor compatible. They are as opposite as yes and no, good and bad, and black and white.

As seen in the Scriptures, God is light and therefore He cannot behold darkness (John 1). As such, God's purpose would have become inefficacious if He had delivered Jesus. Nevertheless, it would also be a sign of weakness and defeat for God to bow or yield to Jesus' cry, even though Jesus was His Son. Jesus had to win the battle on His own, since His mission reveals the fundamental difference of being a victor and a victim. Likewise with the children of Israel, God could not cover or pass over them without the blood being applied. The Bible says *"Love covers over a multitude of sins"* (1 Peter 4:8, NIV). This is the source of how the Lord's power becomes transfigured, and serves to be the birth channel for character and the ignition for purity. Upon such declaration, the same is interpreted today to remind us that God only sees us through Jesus' blood. The defining reference to divine Love is seen through Love, and this is why God sees us through the Love of Jesus. In reference to God's Love, this is one of the reasons why Paul also tells us to present our bodies as a living sacrifice, holy and acceptable to God, which is our reasonable service (Romans 12:1–3).

It is amazing how Jesus redeemed us from sin. With His blood, He presented us to His Father in Love. The primary reason is simple but profound, as God cannot operate outside of His nature—Love. Jesus could not present us to God with goats and bullocks because the substances of deliverance were not therein, as they represented the fruitless power of law and not grace. By this manifestation, we know that there is greater power in Jesus' death over law, as it shows forth a new era by which grace came and established us as joint heirs to the Lord's throne. Thus, Jesus led captive captives by destroying the strongholds between man and law.

As He showed us the symbol of His Love, He also revealed the true meaning of the power of His propitiation; by canceling every death sentence, embarrassment, harassment and disgrace over our life that was designed to bind us in chain of judgment and terror of fear. Now it is over, because through Jesus, our restoration is made whole from the bondage of slavery, both in heaven and on earth. Such restoration, the gospel of Christ has enlisted us into the Kingdom of light, living the light of holiness; teaching the light of purity, and serving with love our brothers and sisters. Through these wonderful mediums, we were presented by Jesus to God as His efficacious blood demonstrated greater power and greater love by which we are divinely covered. And so, before we could have access to the throne of grace, Jesus' blood speaks of a better covenant with God that gave us hope in Christ. This is like wrapping a gift to be presented to a Loved one. We were aliens to God without hope, but through the Lord's Love, we are made right with His Son, Jesus Christ, as seen in Ephesians 2:12 and Colossian 1:21. Praise the Lord for His mercy truly endures forever!

In the same way, our works will never be acceptable unto the Father through Jesus Christ if the essence of His command is absent. Love is the answer and revelation to the heart of God, through Jesus, who prepares the hearts of men to meet face to face with God. As in the Old Testament, before the priest could meet face to face with God, he had to cover himself with the blood of lambs (Hebrews 5). He had to prepare himself prior to going into the Holy of Holies. By comparing the ministry of the priest's life, as it relates to Loving God; to be acceptable in His presence, the ministry of God's Love has to play the same role in our lives.

The ladder of Jacob is another transformation example that demonstrates the principle of Love that leads to the gateway of heaven. To enter into the paradise of heaven is of paramount importance as being born again and is the only way. The Love of God is comparable to Jacob's ladder in conjunction with being born again. Jacob's ladder denotes the connection between heaven and earth with God taking the initiative to reach out to man.

An ideal example is the figure of Jesus who came to earth from the line of Jacob through the provision of God to redeem man so that we may live in heaven for eternity. He was the perfect ladder who was willing to share His saving grace with humanity (John 1:15). This royal step represents the throne of God's Love on which we were rescued through the Love of Christ.

Many schools of thoughts teach that this ladder Jacob saw was a symbol of the ascension of man, progressing from grace to grace until the goal of returning to the Father was achieved. It was a symbolic journey where each of the rungs of the ladder were crucial steps that needed to be taken to move upward in this process. This could be, but one thing is sure, the ladder of Jacob reminds us of another journey, which is the road to eternity. Whether or not we believe this, the way of the cross leads home. And therefore Jacob's ladder leads somewhere too. May your ladder lead to the highway of holiness—or to another place of uncertainty, but if we don't know which way we are going that is saying something about our relationship with God.

That much said, the ladder of Jacob is a significant evidence of God's continual provision for the people in the then, now, and the afterlife. Why? This revelation emphasizes God's willingness to provide for humanity, on earth as well as in the recreation of a new heaven and earth to come. Furthermore, the explicit meaning of Jacob's dream shared the Lord's resurrection in the great communion of saints who have gone before us with the signs of faith and Love. Thus, the ladder came to be seen by Christians as representing that link between heaven and earth which binds the cord of Love with God which cannot be broken. On this account, our hearts become one with the heart of God and the saints whom we eagerly wait to celebrate with.

This is an important message for us today as it relates to the angels traveling both ways on the ladder. It is simple because God's messengers seen going up and down represent the Lord's outstretched Love and grace to the souls of men who will come unto Him. He desires all those who are heavy laden, to come and enjoy the full glory of heaven. Just as the messengers brought help to Jacob in the dream, so the Love of Jesus, represents our requests "going to Jacob's ladder—God's throne of grace." This is a mandate for all of us in Christ to remember. Man must climb up one level at a time to the standard of God's requirements, as he participates in the saving principles and Love of the gospel, offered by the Lord. Who stands at the top to welcome us home into glory? Jesus, the only wise God who became the first fruit of them that slept. It is worth mentioning that as Jacob entered into a covenant with the Lord, he heard the same words of God that were uttered to his grandfather Abraham, and his father Isaac:

And, behold, the Lord stood above it, and said, I am the Lord God of Abraham thy father, and the God of Isaac: the land whereon thou liest, to thee will I give it, and to thy seed; And thy seed shall be as the dust of the earth, and thou shalt spread abroad to the west, and to the east, and to the north, and to the south: and in thee and in thy seed shall all the families of the earth be blessed. And, behold, I am with thee, and will keep thee in all places whither thou goest, and will bring thee again into this land; for I will not leave thee, until I have done that which I have spoken to thee of..
—Genesis 28:13–15, KJV

By contrast, this covenant relationship is also a direct answer to the request Isaac made of the Lord, when he pronounced the blessing on Jacob at the time of his departure from Canaan. We are given clues to the heart of God in reference to Jacob's blessings. In fact, the more we climb the spiritual mountain of God, is the more we will 'be like Him.' That is to be like Christ-like, having the mind of Christ in every sense of the word; as this position places us far above the principalities and powers of this world (Ephesians 1:21). From this lofty spiritual height, we experience greater blessings, greater manifestations, greater transformations, and greater transfigurations, by which the illuminating power of His Love empowers us to tread upon serpents and scorpion and to exercise dominion over the nation and the kingdom of this world (Jeremiah 1:10). This experience should be emulated and practiced by every Christian leader if we are going to triumph over spiritual wickedness in high places.

It is important, moreover, that we look beyond the physical ladder of Jacob and discern the spiritual significance of this ladder, in reference to the mountain transfiguration mentioned by Jesus, Elijah, Moses, David, Caleb and other key leaders in the Bible, that we stay spiritually in this high level of holiness, so that we can be 'caught up to meet Him in the air' when Christ comes to rapture the Church (1 Thessalonians 4:16–17). Elijah prayed down fire and rain from Mount Carmel and singlehandedly changed and defeated the prophets of Baal (1 Kings 18:19–46); Caleb took Mount Hebron at eighty-five years old and militantly fought the giants, thus taking the mountains as God's promise unto him (Joshua 14:7–12). These acts summed up the power of their Love for God. These men of God were 'Love Chasers,' for the holiness of God; thus it is safe to conclude that in an effort and desire to become lovers of the Mountain of God, the Love for holiness is not an option but a standard already designed by God should we decide to come closer to the light by climbing step by step.

Jesus took three of the apostles (Peter, James and John) up into a high mountain. There, He was transfigured before them (Mark 9:2–10). Jesus always went up to the top of the mountain to pray, which is the solution to continued revelation when He ministered. This desire was expressed in His prayer for the church, when He said:

> *Father, I desire that they also, whom You gave me maybe with me*
> *where I am, that they may behold my glory, which You have given*
> *me: for you loved me before the foundation of the world…*
> —John 17: 24, NKJV

We need to come up to the high mountain of perfection in holiness, (2 Corinthians 7:1–2; Hebrews 6:1–2), as well as to come up to the high mountain of righteousness in love since perfect love cast out all fear and in order to sit together with Christ 'in heavenly places' (Ephesians 1:3). However, not every 'Christian' will 'be where he is,' in eternity. Only those who have overcome and who have been living holy lives will live where He is now with Him in heaven (Revelation 3:21). Thus, we should be holy as He is holy, walk as He walked (1 John 2:6), pray as He did, be meek as He also was, Love as He Loved and forgive as He forgave. The Apostle Paul admonishes us to have the mind of Christ, when he says:

Let this mind be in you, which was also in Christ Jesus: Who, being in the form of God, thought it not robbery to be equal with God: But made himself of no reputation, and took upon him the form of a servant, and was made in the likeness of men: And being found in fashion as a man, he humbled himself, and became obedient unto death, even the death of the cross..
—*Philippians 2:5–8, KJV*

The ultimate aim of Christian life is Christ-likeness; that is, to be the like Christ, to be *"conformed to the image"* of Christ (Romans 8:29, ESV), and to radiate His beauty, compassion and holiness.

From this same ladder, Jacob experienced the great reflection of God's likeness, light, wisdom and purpose for his life. Furthermore, God showed him his future seed in contrast with and symbolic to the four corners of the earth. Jacob saw the fascinating end product of Israel's future to come. As noted also, even though God revealed Israel's future to the Old Testament fathers, the promise of being with Jacob was not violated. God was with Jacob as promised, to bring him into the land of his inheritance, and not to rest until it was completed.

God, the same today as yesterday, will never leave us on the ladder of Jacob. His promises are too precious to be forfeited. The requirements of advancing on Jacob's ladder are experienced at the depth and height of God's Love. God's Love is a prototype of climbing a mountain, as in reference to Moses on Mount Sinai, Elijah on Mount Carmel and Caleb on Mount Heron.

Jacob's ladder is figurative to one climbing the mountain of God, and is characterized with making progressive sanctification in God, according to 1 Peter 1:5–6: *"And beside this, giving all diligence, add to your faith virtue; and to virtue knowledge; and to knowledge temperance; and to temperance patience; and to patience godliness"* (1 Peter 1:5–6, KJV). The phrase can also be used interchangeably when referring to the *"Deep calleth unto deep"*

(Psalm 42:7a, KJV) of God's Love and *"Come up hither, and I will shew thee things which must be hereafter"* (Revelation 4:1c, KJV), since as we climb in God's Love, we will experience spiritual perfection and will attain spiritual maturity. This is quite overwhelming as our souls await the final eternal rest in heaven. It is a wonderful experience climbing the ladder of God's Love, as it gives us greater hope, by reason of knowing the heart of God. And thus, it also prepares the soul with different levels of peace as we enter into the arms of Christ, like the poor one experienced in Psalm 34. That is a faithful promise to everyone who believes. Such faithfulness is love. Such Love is like the bridegroom who is waiting for his bride to walk down the aisle, in conjunction with the unfolding purpose of Jacob's ladder. At the top of the ladder of Jacob is Christ along with the arms of Abraham that enfold our hearts into His heart.

We call to mind the transformation of Lazarus' life as it connotes the transaction of divine Love. Lazarus had an encounter with the arms of Christ while he was on earth. As we know, he was poor and neglected by others but never forsaken by Jesus' promises. As he continued on the path of poverty, he had one thing above all gold and riches: a relationship with the heart of God. With this relationship, Lazarus' life was mystically transformed by being accepted and then transported into the arms of Abraham. This, my brothers and sisters, is "Love lifted me" and "from the miry clay" by transferring Lazarus' membership into heaven. Upon such transfiguration, Love is seen as the unbroken circle of a better home awaiting us, in the bye and bye. Such blissful joy provides eternal life, and as well connects us to the throne of God's heart. This is the greatest gift to the world. However, there are but few who Love the Lord's operative principles, but this does not change the government of God's standard unto righteousness, holiness and perfection. His way is holiness, which is above the measure of compromising and man's ways of doings. It does not matter how excellent, authoritative, and famous we are; unless the word of God is the final declaration that solemnly defines His order then the Lord's ways are not truth and righteousness.

God is the author of Love. His very nature is Love. Therefore, we need the unmerited Grace of the Lord's Love to persevere through adversity (2 Corinthians 4:8–10). Thus, since this world is contagious with demonic spirits, such as fear, jealousy, witchcraft, strongholds, diabolic forces, hatred, etc. Christians need to share the Love of God with others, if we are going to conquer and cast out all fears. We should let them know the Love and the hope that salvation brings in Christ. In seeking to get the attention of God, we may seem to be aliens, only if we refuse from acknowledging His reason for being the season of this world.

As we look at Job's life as similar to ours today, we will see the real picture of what I am saying. Love has a role to play in everyone's life. That is rescuing the perishing, and caring for the dying. Although Job was going through his "night process," the role of God's Love was there with him. You see, a night process is a foundational examination requirement designed to give us the proper attitude and the proper effort to grow as a child of God as we develop a personal relationship with the Word of God, through trials, intensified battles, personal setback and running the race to win. As it describes our spiritual experience, in so doing, it gives also gives us basic principles for spiritual growth that further prepare us, by shaping us to serve better spiritually.

This was important for Job, as he maintained his focus, his faithfulness and his relationship with the promises he remembered from God. By trusting totally on the providence of God, he waited humbly on the timetable of God's purpose to unveil itself. Job had no other choice but to surrender to the Lord. Each battle Job encountered gave him an inner hope to capitalize on God's Love. Although Job could not predict his healing, Love consoled him with one of the greatest notions: *"Though after my skin worms destroy this body, yet in my flesh shall I see God"* (Job 19:26, KJV*).* When all other gifts fail, Love will continue. Job had the assurance of God's Love, as stated in the word of God: *"For your shame ye shall have double; and for confusion they shall rejoice in their portion: therefore in their land they shall possess the double: everlasting joy shall be unto them."* (Isaiah 61:7, KJV).

Job never cursed God, even though his condition was heartbroken. Instead, his Love for God never betrayed his faith. As noted prior, Love is the condition of obedience and covenant. Pressing on, Job remarkably held to his integrity in God. His purpose in life was not in the majority of his children but rather in his covenant and obedience to God. The token of Job's Love for God is a transfiguration of Jesus' Love for us. We should be reminded that, each test comes to make us stronger. Indeed, Love is given to preserve us as we walk with God. And Love is given to unite us with God. Can you imagine the complete chaos there would be, without the Love of Jesus (1 Corinthians 15:19)?

THE GRACE OF HIS LOVE MAKES US ACCEPTABLE

The affection of Love is natural, but the Grace of God's Love is transformational. By nature, it is a natural inclination to encounter temptations, but to grossly hate God, or a brother is not divine but demonic. Those who do, fear God, but do not Love Him, because their hearts are challenged by Satan to become desperately wicked. Likewise, when no ordinances, no judgment, or even angels can influence their heart to Love God, this is called a stronghold, as the heart is demonized with deceits. It is only the invincible power of God that can infuse Love in the souls of men after they are delivered. Therefore, we should not let dysfunctional thoughts get in our heart. It is better to talk about them in prayer to Jesus.

Can you imagine if we never experienced the Lord's Love–the grace of Love? Then we would become like Cain and Abel, Jacob and Esau, David and Absalom and of course, haters of God. But God, through His infinite Love, rescues us from the venom of Satan's strongholds.

You see, the Lord looks at Love differently from the human perspective. Love is understood by many as a duty to serve, but in God's eyes, Love is a commitment to serve by transformation expressions. It is not how much we do, but how much we Love. Therefore, if the servant does not do his work willingly with Love, it will not be acceptable. Duties that are not oriented with Love are as burdensome to God as they are to us. An example is David and Solomon, David counseled his son to serve with a willing mind (1 Chronicle 28:9–10). According to Thomas Nelson, "to do duty without Love is not a sacrifice, but penance."[13]

Love is a beautiful flame kindled from heaven; by it, we resemble God, who is Love. Believing or obeying does not make us look like God; it is ultimately by Loving that we will grow like Him and become like Him. It is delighting to God when we can Love, in words and later express Love to others. This is most delightful to God, especially when our words become the fragrance of His Love to others and is accepted by the unsaved. The presence of good traits (Love, peace, joy and longsuffering) is normally given to maintain spiritual growth, and therefore to promote healthy relationship as one cultivates these fruits, his sacrifice will become acceptable unto God.

---

13 Thomas Watson, "All Things for Good," 88, http://lifeisworship.com/tag/Love/

Love flows joyfully when it helps to free one of pain and hatred

Above everything, the most common denominator that was outstanding in Jesus' ministry on earth was Love. Love characterized Jesus' life, personhood and ministry. Every opportunity Jesus had He offered Love in a positive way to the crowd in conjunction with His Father's Love. Through this avenue, Jesus captured their attention with Love. Even when many had only a vague description of His teachings, He never sought to foster hatred in His heart against them. Instead, He interacted with the people, and wisely knew their hearts as He comforted their beliefs and doubts with signs and wonders. As they struggled to maintain optimism, Jesus faithfully administered His Father's will, the Love of God. Avoiding traditional approaches, doctrines of the devil and confrontational soul winning objectives, Jesus humbly changed the subject of their argument with the spirit of prayer and the spirit of Love, as He discovered the deceitfulness of their hearts. Compassion and friendship characterized Jesus' Love for people. He met their needs and then they wanted to follow Him.

When we are showing Love, we do not have to defend ourselves. Love is a lifestyle. While other attributes are leaning on lies, its oath and covenant is supported with the righteousness of God, not on 'sinking sand' but instead with an anchor of truth that grips the solid rock of Jesus' blood and righteousness. It does not practice fables before the throne of grace or demonstrate babbling personalities among others. Yes, it does one thing: it stands on the power and authority, the *exousia* of truth, by supporting honesty only, and by showing righteousness greatly, while standing on the foundation of Christ, rejoicing. These religious sects were offended by Jesus' teachings. Jesus, nonetheless, shared the Love of His Father's commandments courageously and extensively with them. Genuine Love will never leave you out.

Not everyone will respond to our teachings. Only the intensity of the word with Love will do the conviction. Thus we should let Love does the work where there is no evaluation. With the evidence of Jesus' Love seen in us and on the ministry, hearts will be transformed.

How can someone deny the Love of Christ, when they were born in the Love of Christ? There is one possible answer, and that is pride. Pride is the root of sin. Sin is the son of Satan and Satan is the father of sin as well. To be driven with stomach hatred is not light but darkness transfigured.

Stomach hatred is an internal stronghold rooted with maximum envious thoughts. Hatred only sends us on a desperate road, struggling with sadness, entertaining negative mindsets and replaying evil unforgiving thoughts, by looking for evidence to accuse innocents. But, the beauty of having Love is that it leads to mercy:

- Love understands the pain and struggles we have been going through. Therefore, its divine promises to us are sure and ever truthful. By helping us to get back on the road of joy, and by reinstating us with the medal of joy once lost with others, but not in Christ, is the unmerited agenda of Love, divine Love.

- Love only wraps His arms around the past and elatedly restores the spirit of joy unto us.

It is Christ's Love that brings such amazing connection that makes our words, our services and our relationship become acceptable and profound. When conditions look hopeless, we are to praise Him each day. When the opportunity presents itself, we are to praise Him more joyfully; by doing this, God's grace will fulfils the desires of our hearts. Moreover, like a stream of gladness, Jesus will be there at all times and as a means to assure us of His promises unto our children's children. Should you have not known, we are embraced with His Love and daily loaded with His benefits, " *"Blessed be the Lord, Who daily loadeth us with benefits even the God of our salvation..."* (Psalm 68:19, KJV). We are labeled with the victory of grace, as Love overpowers law and death, by which we are made the instruments of God's Love.

Love is the power of now and is the covenant on which all hopes and all blessings are confirmed within the Scriptures. Such confirmation is seen in Numbers:

> *The Lord bless you and keep you; The Lord make His face shine upon you, And be gracious to you; The Lord lift up His countenance upon you, And give you peace.*
>
> —Numbers 6:24–26, NKJV

Therefore the words of our mouth are the harmony of the heart, in which worship in spirit and truth is also accomplished in righteousness. This is what makes the heart of man become acceptable unto God.

In the context of Psalm 19:14, the heart is used by God to illustrate its deception. But the heart also holds the most secret things and is the most powerful organ when it is in operation with the harmony of the words of God to transform behavioral patterns. (See Colossians 3 and Philippians 4:8.)

Likewise the psalmist's words were not matching his heart; perhaps he was not acknowledging the submerged thoughts in his heart. So, he realized it was time to re-take an inventory of his life. In response to the scenarios of his heart, he was able to resolve the condition of his heart as a means of getting his life and words in harmony with his heart.

For our heart to remain spotless and to find God's soulmate for our life, our life should undergo spiritual surgery that is transformation, by which the Holy Spirit becomes the beacon of light in our life. This will keep the heart safe from submerging morass growing from within. Such experience is transforming and therefore has the power to bring us into a new light of knowledge, of what it means to intercede with prayer and to soak our self into His word wholly.

The moment we stop fighting for each other is the moment we will lose our humanity. Jesus is calling us. We can achieve the impossible. Try Jesus! He believes in us. Thus He believes we are capable to be the best. Jesus Loves us very much. His promises are yes and amen. Therefore, we will not go through the symptoms of stress again. Today is our day. Yes, Jesus is our support in the whelming flood. His presence is always with us, and in His heart the answer is yes. We will be the golden winner to our family. Jesus Loves us above and beyond any other design. His promises are yes and amen; because of this, our personal life will never be affected by deceit anymore.

Love is the only fundamental truth ever shared and thus articulated by the world's theism that has defined the continuity of God's existence. By contrast, inasmuch as other discoveries have impacted the world, no other to date has ever taken the role of the creating deity. No other religion has ever taken the initiative to return from the fruit of the ground as Jesus did, by conveying the message of Love, hope and light to humanity. As one continues to look even deeper into the significance of Christ in you, the hope of glory (Colossians 3:16), the fullness of His manifestations will become apparent as we practice and appreciate His presence. In like manner, the previous hidden mystery of God's intimate initiative is absolutely astir in our hearts to respond with gratefulness. Certainly, such conviction is piercing as we recall the invited loving call of God's salvation. This indeed is the birth of spiritual transformation.

God's initiative is a significant reflection of His Love. He has taken the initiative to express His Love when He breathed into man. Through this avenue, man's spirit became a living soul. After which, he also became the activity of God's image of what he is today. On this account, as man sought God through the illuminated knowledge of God, he recognized his responsibility to the world and to his God. Here his soul became acquainted with the meditation of his heart as he partook either in the pleasure of sin or in the perpetual things of God. To be acceptable in the chamber of God's presence, man's life has to be transformed from within if he so desires to walk in the meditation of the word of the Lord (see Psalm 1).

You see, our emotional attachments within creation clearly show God's compassion. Man was made in the reflection of God's image. This describes the mystery of man's productive spirit being a source directly from God, which makes man into a composite of the nature, attributes, and character of the maker. We were made unconditionally before God in the eternity counsel of the godhead. We were purposed, preordained, elected and chosen as His workmanship, until sin damaged the relationship of unconditional covenant to a covenant of condition, where man is now given a promise that is primarily governed by His obedience.[14] We are not the image of any other creation, except the creator of Love, the Lord's Love.

God is an emotional spirit. He is loaded daily with passion and compassion for us. In the faith of the Buddhist, their expression of compassion is attached with passion, meaning active concern, sympathy and a willingness to bear the pain or the burden of another. The Buddhist demonstrates deep compassion and in fact, believes they were placed on the earth to show compassion. Such attributes embody the compassion of servanthood and therefore demonstrate the first and last mentioned principle through the Bible—Love.

---

14 Merits Henry, "The Anointing Exposes the Deeds of the Flesh" (Bloomingston: Westbrow Press, 2011), 11.

Much can be said in this light, but are we at the level of the Buddhist in showing compassion? The dynamic of Jesus' ministries were surrounded with Love, compassion and friendship. Jesus was sensitive and selective to the needs of the people as He effectively reached out to them. Our Love should draw others to us and Christ, not only by our giving, but also with our fellowshipping (Ephesians 4:11–16). The function of every part of the body is to cause growth and to edify itself in Love. Therefore a revelation of the body, both spiritual and physical is paramount for success. How can a person Love His body and not Love others? This is not Love. This is obsessional pride.

The Love of Christ was in existence long before any converts were brought into it. Therefore, as human beings, it is our responsibility to become givers of compassion, for we are said to be made in the image of compassion. In God's image, there is absolutely no degree of demerit. Can you imagine, there is no irrevocable invocation relating to the apparent nature of God's existence? Because, His unfolding nature is His Love and His unfolding nature is His grace towards us. This is Love, Love for the souls of humanity (Romans 11). And so, this is the primary difference between religion and relationships. Religion is a set of rules that is based on philosophy and ideology, while relationship is having a spiritual craving; having a spiritual response within through the channel of the Holy Spirit, in which the inner man is satisfied with the indescribable longing and feeling of one's pursuit.

The very nature of such immortal existence further reveals the never changing immutable truth about God. True discernment is wrapped up in His Love. Therefore, we must first find the heart of God, which is Love. This is the heart of God and above all, this is the voice of God. The voice of God is calling out unto man through different revelations. The realization of these inspiring thoughts, today has actively expressed Love, and has laid the foundation of brotherhood and inner unity. Among such expressions is compassion. Compassion is first, the very basic nature and truth of God's existence. On this divine inscription is founded the deepest and greatest sacrifice ever demonstrated by Jesus (John 3:16).

The lesson of Psalm 19 exposes the weakness of religion against the message of consolation in Jesus Christ. The psalmist reveals the deepest desires of the heart of man in such a spiritual way that it will rearrange his thinking patterns, empower his life, and as well as allow him to discover the truth of genuine servitude. As we flip through the pages of our lives, may we ultimately enter into a deeper relationship with God; and may we discover the Love of God, which is meant for us. This way, we will understand the true meaning of divine Love, as it was prophesied two thousand years ago.

When all is said and done, words are still the essence of creation. Love on the other hand is still the motivation for creation. When God created the world, He wisely used specific words to impregnate the vision. That vision then produced hope, love and faith. Through such medium of His expression we are created in His image. With an emblem of purpose and love for destiny, we become the centerpiece of His creative motivation. By such provision made with His Son, Jesus Christ, His heavenly authorities extended godly grace to our hearts. Thus, within this invitation, our souls discovered the source of private and public devotions as our human soul cries for moments of impact, purpose, and significance. Here we experience the voice of God calling us by name to let the words of our mouth and the meditation of His will be acceptable in us.

It is imperative as we present our different gifts to God to bear in mind, the message within this book. Apart from the pure doxology of Love, words are meant to stand as an advocate for the unloved. Love and words are pertinent, as its responsibilities are to hold our inner desires, our inner thoughts, and most sacred wishes above all things. We should know that words will come and words will go. But, what matters most is the condition of the heart, as it will either disrupt others, disgrace oneself or elevate us to be acceptable unto God. Therefore, let us rest assured by embracing the truth and the meditation of His Word from a pure heart of Love. As thoughts generated from a heart of Love will be acceptable unto God when He comes. Thus, let us live the Word of God and be prepared to move from glory to glory

WALK THROUGH

Dear Jesus,

May my heart dwell in its secret springs and let my words flow with Love.

Lord, help me to find Your Love so that I can allow others to experience You. It is my desire to share You with my neighbors. It is my greatest aim to help others discovering the sacred places of Your heart. God I want to dwell there with You, Oh God! There in safety, peace, serenity, harmony, tranquility, and above all Love in You.

Let me earnestly persuade all who bear the name of Christ to become like You. Lord, I know that Love is the incense which makes all our services become an acceptable fragrance.

Amen!

SUMMARY AND REFLECTION

1. We were made _____ before God in the eternity counsel of the Godhead until _____ changedthe relationship of unconditional covenant to a covenant of condition.

2. In reference to Cain's offering, there was much evidence as to why his offering was rejected by God. Can you name the main reason as noted in *Love Reveals the Heart of God*, why Cain's offering was rejected?

   _____

3. For our gifts to be connected to the Throne of Grace, what are two ways, we can practice the Love of God, as it resonates in our hearts?

   a) _____
   b) _____.

4. True or False? Love is a beautiful flame kindled from heaven; by it we resemble God, who is Love. _____

5. Dr. Stephen Covey believes that we all have a _____ Account that is only active or alive when daily deposits are made. Another name for "Love tank" is _____ that is paralleled to lasting and effective relationship with _____ and _____.

6. Explain the paraphrase, "the water of repentance is not pure, unless it flows from the spring of genuine Love."_____

_____

_____

7. True or False? Love is to do everything God does. _____

8. Apart from Moses, which other Old Testament leader in particular, taught the greatest commandment of God as referred in Luke 10:27?

_____

9. True or False? Worldly things will die and leave us but the Love of God is forever. _____

EVALUATION AND TEMPERAMENT

1. Self-examination is the core inspector of the heart. Many times we may perceive others wrongly and also try to resolve things differently. If you have experienced countless accusations by one of your bosses or associates, and you are uncertain as to how to deal with the situation, what steps could you take to be selective in your approach?

2. Please explain your choice of preference selected above.

_____

_____

_____

_____

3. When I speak the words that matter most, I am speaking the words that fit mostly my vocabulary with God, and my self-esteem. Can you

recall any trying moments when you had to put self aside and let the Spirit of God take pre-eminence in the situation? If your answer is yes, please explain; and describe how you felt after.

_____

_____

_____

_____

4. Write down some of your goals for family along with your expectations. Be honest and share one with your spouse.
   Goals:

   _____

   _____

   _____

   _____

5. If you are married or are in a relationship and you realize that your Love tank is running low, or perhaps like Job you are just losing everything around you, write down at least three things that could have be a factor at home.

   a) _____

   b) _____

   c) _____

6. Write down at least one internal thought that you can use to pursue the presence of God more and that will enhance a greater union of Love at home. _____

7. Write down some external qualities you admire about your service to God and family.

   _____

   _____

   _____

   _____

8. If the home is not characterized by Love and there are frozen feelings circulating in the air, how could you resolve, relinquish and rebuild from the lesson of Psalm 19?

a) _____

b) _____

c) _____

d) _____

LOVE REQUEST

Name the things that are missing from your life that you would like to experience to be at peace with yourself and also most importantly with Jesus in relation to the above lesson.

Write down three words of supplication that you would like to see manifested, reaffirmed and resolved in your life, family and friendships.

_____

_____

_____

Since it was on Calvary that he made the greatest display of his Love for us; be not like those, who give themselves to Him at one season, and withdraw from him at another. Instead, let us consider one another to provoke unto Love and to good works.

Love Reveals the Heart of God

The soul that possess a warm affection to God and others is distinguished above danger or fear, shall dwell in peace and find rest within the secret place of God.

"Because he hath set his Love upon me,
therefore will I deliver him: I will set him on high,
because he hath known my name."

—Psalm 91:14, KJV

CHAPTER FOUR

Shadowed In The Depth Of His Love

Have you ever been disappointed by the promises that others made to you? Have you ever felt as if your life is just somewhat slowly slipping by, leaving in its wake many unfulfilled dreams and broken promises? If your answer to these questions is yes, then ask yourself: who hasn't? I too had felt dejected, disillusioned and abandoned by those who had faithfully promised to be there for me in my time of need. I trusted them; I believed in their false promises of opening doors for me so that I could easily slide through them. But, at the end, all my hopes had been shattered by their broken promises and by their rejections, leaving me feeling dejected, alone and hopeless. You see, I had placed my hopes, my dreams and my beliefs in the words of my fellow *man* instead of placing my trust in the true promises of God. Nevertheless, throughout all of my despair and throughout all of my feelings of abandonment, I was made to draw closer to the Lord, the God of my salvation—The Lord who has never broken His promises to me, the God whose promises are sure.

During my hours of despair, I was constantly reminded, by the Word of the Lord, to refocus my trust and my beliefs only on the promises of Jesus Christ. Remembering that the Lord has promised that He would *never leave me neither would He ever forsake me*, just as He had in His promise to His servant David at the time when David felt as if all his hopes had been lost. David acknowledged God's promises as he was inspired by the Lord to write these words: *"... he hath set his Love upon me, therefore will I deliver him, I will set him on high because he hath known My Name"* (Psalm 91:14, KJV). Just like David, I have taken comfort in the promises of the Almighty, knowing that He will never falter on the promises that He made to me when I first accepted Him as my loving Savior. I now realize that all I have to do is to believe His Word and trust in His faithful promises as David did.

As a young pastor, I trusted in the promises of others, and they abandoned me on the highway of despair; those to whom I had relied on for guidance had left me with shattered dreams and broken promises. But God, in His mercy allowed me to recognize that my hope cannot be built on the promises of human kindness, and neither can it be built on the dreams and aspirations of others, but my hope is built only on the divine promises of Almighty God, a God whose promises are sure.

Had I lost my focus on the Lord when I allowed myself to be misled by the promises of man? Yes. But in my hurt and disappointment, I was reminded to call on my Lord saying: *Lord where Art Thou?* Then the Lord heard me and reminded me that my help comes only from Him, the Lord (Psalm 121). The impact of God's presence in my life is an unprecedented disclosure as declared in Psalm 91: *"...He hath set His Love upon me...."*(Psalm 91:14, KJV).

As I roll back the curtain of my life and glimpse where the Lord has brought me from, I see the veil that once blinded my eyes to God's Love, and to the hope of His salvation. Then when the veil was fully removed to reveal the true mystery of God's divine will for me, I not only saw clearly the works of His hand in my life, and experience the power of His divine Love for me, but I was able to see the reflection of who I really am, as a human being and as a child of God. I was also able to discover the deceptive nature of the human race.

One morning, during one of my deepest moments of despair, as I knelt alone in prayer and supplication before the Almighty, I cried: *"Lord, please forgive me for my folly, and give me the grace to restore my faith in you, as I need your guidance to make it through."* At that very moment, I could hear His sweet, small voice whispering to me: *"You are being tested."* Upon hearing His voice, I cried out even more, *"Lord I'm broken-hearted, and I need your grace to surround me. I know that I'm unworthy but I do know that you are always listening to your children's cry."* There, at that very moment, I sensed His presence in my spirit as He whispered: *"My peace is upon you, my son. I allowed this situation to take place in your life because I do Love you."* Was this voice real? I asked myself. I came to the realization, that yes, it was the voice of the Lord speaking to me. In my darkest hour, when everyone had forsaken me, *"He was there all the time, waiting for me to surrender to his will, just waiting to hide me in his own secret place."* Yes, He was just waiting for my call; waiting for me to surrender to His will.

I was shadowed with the Love of the Lord, the Love which brings me peace during my moments of despair, the Love that is worth more than the false promises of men to me. In other words, I felt relieved when I heard and experienced the sweet melodious voice of the Lord. Oh, the voice of the Lord makes all the difference! The wings of His Love embraced my heart with the distinction of His voice. What an aura it is! To be overshadowed with the great power and security of a loving Savior! His Love lifted me that morning, providing a refuge for my broken spirit, as I anchored my soul in the depth of His Love. It was the most refreshing feeling of peace that I had ever experienced. I was now able to take responsibility for my feeling of complacency; for putting my trust in the promises of men; as His loving voice empowered me; as His mighty arms embraced me; and as His tender mercy restored and led me to attain greater heights in Him.

As children of God, we are sometimes faced with many hard choices, but the Lord does allow us to make our own choice. He allows us to go through situations, depending on the choice that we have made. However, like a mother's arms protecting her children from danger, so it is that God overshadows His children with His Love; in the arms of the Lord is a place of protection from the enemy. As the psalmist declares, *"He shall cover thee with his feathers and under His wings you will find refuge"* (Psalm 91:4, NIV).

There is a place of safety that we must find as believers, and it is in the Lord. As believers we must come to know and experience personally, *'that secret place of God's Love,'* remembering that God's abiding peace is that place of rest where His Love lies; and it is in the overflow of His grace.

Whenever we are faced with our trials, our only hope is in the Lord, because He is the one who really cares. He hears our cry and He also answers our requests. In the darkest moments of our life, He will reveal His Love to us. We must remember that it was in the dark clouds that Moses met the Lord face to face, and that was where he gained favor with the God of his fathers. Also it was in the dark clouds that Moses gained mercy and favor with the Lord (Exodus 24:18). As God's children, let us not be afraid of the dark clouds, for in the dark clouds we will find the shadow of His protection and His Love.

We need not worry about our future, because our future is in the hands of the Lord; we must take care only to abide under the shadow of His almighty wings. There is where our future and our safety lie; that is where the place of refuge is; and there is where we find shelter from the evil one. As we look deeper into the secret place of God's Love, we will discover Jesus' divine protection for us. So, let us not grow weary when life becomes a winding road, but let us be assured that God has already defined the path and depth through which His Love will take us. We must remember that in Christ there is a place of safety that we will all come to know and experience through His grace. What is that place? That place is under the shadow of God's almighty wings, where His Love flows.

The world can never give to us the genuine Love and peace that we are so hungry for, because the world cannot give what it does not have. But The Lord's tender loving care is ever present with us (Psalm 121). In the depths of His Love, He overshadows His children. Studies have shown that people need eight hugs per day for mental stability; however, this same study reveals that no one is really able to get eight hugs per day. It is only when our lives have been shadowed in the depths of God's Love that we will find the peace that human hugs cannot provide us with. It is in God's Love that we feel secured, because His Love gives us comfort; His Love gives us peace; and His Love gives us the reassurance as it provides us with the hope and protection that we need.

When Lazarus fell into the loving arms of Abraham, how illuminated he must have felt. Is our life being shadowed in the depth of such Love? Oh, just the joy of having the comforting arms of our loving Father surrounding us. We who are the children of the Lord are secured in His Love. It is always so comforting to know that we are protected by the shadow of His wings around us. Yes, it is quite normal for us, at times, to feel insecure, not knowing what God's plan is for our life; but we can be assured, that as His children, we are secured in His everlasting Love, and that He will never fail us. His thoughts and His plans for our life are pure and just.

We must be thankful that we are living under, and in the overflow of such Love. We should be so grateful to be dwelling under the shadow of God's wings! God will always take care of us as the space in His heart is reserved for His children. The landscape of His heart is designated as a mansion to house all of His faithful children. This is true as stated in John 1:14 that we should not allow our hearts to be troubled. We are constantly dwelling in the shadow of God's presence. God has broadened our understanding concerning His Love for us—so that His Love may reveal His heart to us, as stated in Psalm 91.

Before becoming acquainted with the Love of God and with the revelation of the Scriptures, I had always wrestled with the different thoughts that I would normally experience at church, as I wondered if there was not more about the Lord, in the Scriptures, than our projected beliefs. And so, I began to develop a deep hunger and thirst for the revelation of the word of the Lord; and as I searched the Scriptures daily, I discovered that the greatest treasures are hidden within the revealing words. Then I began to understand the revelation of Psalm 91, and also the significance of the other sacred psalms. In essence, their spiritual meanings and benefits have been revealed to me, as I began to learn the importance of the context of each verse in each psalm, and specifically the true meaning of Psalm 91.

Psalm 91 conveys a relationship between God and His people. This relationship between God and us is the one that draws us closer to the Lord, closer than we could ever imagine. It expresses the deep feelings of the hearts, the passions, the desires, and the dreams as it advises us concerning the benefits of the protection and of the true mercies of the Lord. It teaches us that the faithfulness of God's relationship with us will never change; it also reveals to us the relationship between two persons in a mutually agreed on relationship. This is revealed in the close relationship that David had with the Lord, and also in the everlasting Love between the Lord Jesus and us, as His bride in the fourteenth verse of Psalm 91.[15]

This psalm echoes the voice of God as it illustrates the Love of Jesus to the church. Revealing the greatest examples of God's plan, the psalmist further explains God's secrets, His Love and assurance to us. This is seen through Jesus, the Man, as he detailed the destiny of our life. The psalm is prophetic as it reveals the nature of Christ in His incarnation; in His suffering; in His crucifixion; in the rejection of Him by His own people; and in His victory over death. These are the revelations of God's truth, and they are also examples of the holy of holies that have further revealed the mind of Christ.

There are notable testimonies presented that are aligned with our emotions; with our desires; and with our sufferings. Like Jesus Christ, we

---

15 Gill's and Matthew Henry's Exposition of the Bible

must pass through difficult circumstances. But, such circumstances leave us with joyous anticipation which the Lord will reveal through the theme of His heart to us.

Each verse of Psalm 91 reveals mutual responsibility, personal commitment and emotional attachment of human faith; and there is no question as to 'who' will determine man's departure: only the Creator can and will determine the appropriate time of such an event.

The Love of God is the essence of all things; it is absolutely perfect in every way. The Love of God is unconditional, and its supply is limitless. Psalm 91 exhorts the depth of His Love for His children. This is the result of His promise to us: within the shadow of His Love there are intense desires and imaginative thoughts; there is victory that is connected through the verses of this psalm. What an awesome scene this is, as it reveals the secret place of the Most High in all of its glory, in its entire splendor, in all its protection; and in all its affection to us. The psalmist wisely chose his words as he describes the absolute counsel of the shadow of the Almighty. Shadowed in the depth of His Love in verse two of the Psalm, the writer refers to the safety of abiding in the presence of God, as it divinely illustrates the object of administration in our lives. This proven assurance secures our commitment to God through Jesus Christ.

His shadow speaks of His enduring presence and protective feeling of warmth and affection, as experienced, when the newborn is cuddled in the loving arms of its mother. This feeling of Love that is expressed by the psalmist is like that of Lazarus as he was cuddled in Abraham's bosom (Psalm 91:4). While the secret place suggests the promise reserved for His people, this holy feeling is depicted in the heart of the man whom God has set His Love on. Through this blessed hope of eternal salvation, we will enjoy the unfolding secret of shadowing under His wings through His Love.

It is believed that the words spoken in verse one of Psalm 91 are vows expressing the relationship between the Lord and His people. The focus of this psalm is a statement of security, a statement of Love, a statement of relationship and above all, it is a statement concerning the covenant between us and the Father. On such note, God would secure us on the commitment that we have made to Him. His promise is to protect us, but we must remember that the Lord will hold us accountable for violating the terms of our covenant with Him. The promise of His Love is God's commitment to us, but the choice is ours to make (Psalm 91:9–13). Our decision will determine if we will gain access to the grace of God. Nevertheless, the theme of Psalm 91 is built around the characteristics of His Love for us.

God is Love (1 John 4:8). He has expressed His leadership in His Love for His children. Everything He does for us is motivated by His Love towards us. The experiences of the believer in the Lord are delightful and they also symbolize God's glory and holiness. These words in 1 John 4:8 reveal the measure of God's protection and Love for us. Everything to satisfy our desires and to make our soul delight in the Lord is found in the resting care of God's Love towards us. Here is a scene: we are the object of His loving-kindness as He extends the shadow of His wings to protect us. He has set His Love upon us; hence He has removed our sin and has placed it upon Himself so that He could set His Love on us.

Ceaselessly, God has set His Love upon us. With all our hearts we must Love Him, as we find ourselves wrapped in the shadow of His presence with the fullness of having His Joy. Ultimately we should be thankful to be in the presence of the Lord. For in His presence, we surrender to His perfect will, and in the shadow of His secret place, we will live in victory as we walk in confidence, because we are assured that the power of our enemy has been destroyed. The Lord has given us the power over our enemy. We are among those who are seated far above principality and dominion (Ephesians 1:18-20; 2:4-7).

God's revelation to Moses was a symbol of His Love and promise made. Moses understood this revelation as the heart of God moving His people forward into His plan—the Promised Land. Of course, this was the heart of God for the children of Israel. In this psalm, it is the heart of God's Love revealed (Psalm 91:3-8.)

Throughout history, God has been very lenient with the children of Israel. He trained them in the wilderness to establish their trust in Him. God's aim was to reveal to them and to teach them about who He was, so that they would walk with Him in a covenant relationship and thus, by doing so, understand the secret place of His tabernacle. Nevertheless, the decision was theirs to make.

The children of Israel would inherit a land, which was not their own, consisting of milk and honey. This also points to the physical and spiritual transferring of God's inheritance to the children of Israel. It was a land that was prepared and developed for them through the power of God's Love. On the hand, this was a place saturated with rich provision; a place that would bring joy, peace and Love which would enhance their relationship with the Lord, and bring much satisfaction to His people.

God had designed a special place for the Children of Israel that they would be able to call a land of promise. But they would never have seen the secret of God's promise until they decided to abide by the ordinances of God, even though they were told about it by Moses and Joshua. To have a vision is a blessing, but to bring that vision into the promised future and to make that vision a reality, one has to walk by faith and not by sight. Eventually, the children of Israel followed God's command and as a result, God's policy and His Love were revealed to them. On their own, they would not have been able to abide in God's ways. Nothing was more important to the Lord than to develop a loving and understanding relationship with them. In doing so, they would find a place of rest, a place sustained by the presence of the Lord.

WALK THROUGH

Dear Lord,

Thank You for hiding my soul in the cleft of the rock that shadows a dry and thirsty land. My soul panteth for Your rescuing grace and mercy that brought me through each moment of the hour, day, week, month and year. I am living this moment because of Your unfailing Love that saves a sinner like me.

Help me, Lord, to know You more deeply, especially in my darkest hours. To discern between light and darkness, and to know when it is You speaking and not my mind.

You are great! Your manifold wisdom established is from eternity to everlasting. I thank you Lord for being a part of my life. I thank You, Lord, for sheltering me in Your secret place. Your presence has revolutionized my life to another level of desiring You only.

Keep me safe in Your arms like You did with Lazarus in the bosom of Abraham through the precious name of Jesus. Lord, I want to continually abiding under the shadow of the Almighty, to experience the warmth of Your tender Love. I want to be away from the noisome pestilence that walketh in darkness and the destruction at day time.

Thank You, dear Lord, Your divine protection over my life daily is appreciated. Thank You for the necessities that sustain us and that we may obtain mercy and find favor in times of need. You are a mighty God. I most humbly commit myself to you for Your sovereign protection. In my weaknesses, please strengthen me with joy, Grace, and power.

Show me Your Love and faithfulness in my shadows, mysteries, and dreams. Help me to be humble and not to be illuminated by anger, danger and fear. Clear my doubts so that I can transparently see You as light in my darkest hours. In the name of Your Son, Jesus,

Amen.

SUMMARY AND REFLECTION

Complete the following:

1. True or False? The inspired author writes of a secret place wherein men may dwell beneath the shadow of God. He writes of protection, of deliverance from troubles, and of a long and prosperous life. _____

2. True or False? Those who set their Love upon Jehovah God shall reap the reward of a long and honorable life. _____

3. There is much symbolism in the temple. The temple is arranged so that someone coming to the temple must go past a series of objects as he/she draws near to God. Because the primary way that we draw near to God is through prayer, the sequence of petitions in prayer should be patterned after the sequence of objects in the temple. Describe the three dimensions of God's presence and identify the purpose in prayer that each object symbolizes.

   a) The _____ is God's omnipresence and it symbolizes God's presence in all creation.
   b) The inner court is _____ and it symbolizes God's presence in the heart of His people.
   c) The Holy of holies is _____ and it symbolizes _____.

4. The secret of a long and prosperous life is standing in the shadow of_____.

5. True or False? Although the opening of the psalm proclaims a secret place, it only takes a moment for the reader to comprehend that the true source of protection is not a place, but rather it is the person of God.

6. According to the Word of God, except the seed dies it cannot _____

7. Complete the phrase:

   _____ of His _____ is in His Love. Only God gives revelation.

8. Our fragile fate was spiritually seasoned from_____ to _____ in Christ.

9. _____ Love is temporarily engrafted in human heart but the _____ Love of God is imputed in the heart of _____ forever.

10. True or False? The foreknowledge of God has been perfectly defined as His awareness of the decision some people would make to follow Christ, forming the basis of His choice.

11. True or False? It is the immutable precedent that governs our behavior?

   _____

EVALUATION AND TEMPERAMENT

1. You will never reach higher than you are now, never know fulfillment, nor achieve the plan and purpose that God has for you, *unless* you learn to dwell in the Secret Place. Name three benefits of being shadowed in this secret place

   a) _____
   b) _____
   c) _____

2. Why are we distinguished and marked by experiencing a deeper knowledge of God, above danger or fear, where we shall dwell in peace and joy being shadowed in the depth of His Love?

   _____

3. It's about time we all recognize and share our most precious gifts. From the responses below, how do you think this should be done?

a) Moderately
b) Assertively
c) Prayerfully
d) Compulsively
e) Friendly
f) With words of wisdom and Love
g) All of the above

4. List three things that you believe are necessary to embrace the total man

a) _____
b) _____
c) _____

5. How can we make time for the spiritual man to nourish our physical relationship?

LOVE REQUEST

Things that are missing from your life that you would like to experience; to be at peace with yourself and most importantly with Jesus in relation to this lesson.

Write down three words of supplication that you would like to see manifested, reaffirmed and resolved in your life, family and friendships.

_____

_____

_____

Love Reveals the Heart of God

*A sacrifice to be real must cost, must hurt, and must empty ourselves.
Give yourself fully to God. He will use you to accomplish great things
on the condition that you believe much more in his Love than in
your weakness.*

—Mother Teresa

*"For thou possessed my reins:
thou hast covered me in my mother's womb."*

—Psalm 139:13, KJV

CHAPTER FIVE

Framing Love

The psalmist declares God's perfect Love for mankind by stating: *"...marvelous are thy works, and that my soul knoweth right well"* (Psalm 139:14, KJV). This psalm reveals God's Love for us as it relates the different stages of mankind's development. It tells of the intricate thoughts that went into such plan; the Love that unfolded from the heart of the Lord, as He stooped so low in Love to create us. When the psalmist looked at the wonder of the Lord, he again declares that we are fearfully and wonderfully made...and that his soul knows quite well. This reveals the depths of God's Love for mankind, when He fashioned us and shaped us into His own image; after which He then knelt down and breathed His own Spirit within us. 'Oh How He Loves Us.'"

What passion and what Love that exist between the Lord and His people. A new mother is enthused and overwhelmed as she embraces her precious child in her arms, how much more precious are we in the arms of our Lord? He created us in His own image; He formed us with His own hands; and He sent His only Son, Jesus to die a gruesome death on the cross, to redeem us back unto Himself. We are the apples of God's eye, and the only desire of His heart! As the potter designed the clay into unique vessels, how unique we are in the heart of the Lord; we are God's masterpiece; and we are peculiar in His eyes.

God created us; He knows and understands us from afar. The Lord desires an intimate relationship with us because of His Love for us. With careful studying of each verse in Psalm 139, we have discovered all the elements of God's gracious Love for His people. We are convinced that God's relationship with us brings an abundance of understanding and clarity concerning His Love for us. In addition to the understanding of His Love, we are given the ability to relate to one another with grace, with understanding and with the Love of God in our heart.

The home of the believer must display the everlasting Love of God. Such Love must be evident through the various stages of the family's development; the Love of God must be shown in the lives of the believers and must also be displayed in the behavior of their children: "*Train up a child the way he should go; and when he is old he will not depart from it*" (Proverbs 22:6, KJV).

A Christ-like home is a home where the Love of God is actively shown in the lives of the family because the Love of God is the leading factor in creating a stable home environment. This is Framing Love. Framing Love must be the foundation on which the children's characters are built. They must see this foundation as the design and as the plan of the Lord. Framing Love must be a committed desire on which all promises of God's Love are built.

"*...Before I formed you in the womb, I knew you*" (Jeremiah 1:5, NIV) the Lord declared to Jeremiah. Such s statement reveals to us the intent of God's heart towards those to whom He has called to be leaders in His vineyard. This is the uniqueness of framing Love. It refreshes us with the benefits of God's promises. Love was God's passion when He formed us from the dust of the earth.

To bring us to light of His framing Love, He transitions us into an insightful life, a life that is best for us. With a father's Love, He gazes upon us with divine admiration even when we fail. Adam failed, so we also have failed, but yet, He in His Love and mercy, has seen it fit to redeem us back unto Himself, because of His great Love for us. As human beings, we would not allow a life of unhappiness for our children, so therefore the Lord would not have left us to perish after the fall of Adam. As the Scripture declared: "*Greater Love hath no man than this....*" (John 15:13, KJV).

We were designed distinctly to be Loved by the Lord, and as a family, to impart our Love to one another, through the grace of the Lord. "*For God so Loved the world that he gave....*" (John 3:16, ESV). How? He gave His life for us; He is there all the time waiting patiently. These are crucial elements of God's divine covering and provision for His people as His Love is accurately revealed for us through His Son Jesus Christ who gave His life to redeem us back unto His Father.

We are special to God. He has placed within us important principles that will guide us. It is critical that we follow the plan that the Lord has laid out for us; the plan to restore our faith in Him. He knows about us; He formed us; as He declares to Jeremiah: *"Before I formed you in the womb, I knew you"* (Jeremiah 1:5, ESV). The Lord Jesus knows us and He is acquainted with our ways. We are incomplete until we have His indwelling presence within us. We are what matters to our Lord Jesus; He died for us.

The Scripture declares: *"For we are his workmanship, created in Christ Jesus for good works, which God prepared beforehand, that we should walk in them"* (Ephesians 2:10, ESV).

Someone once stated, concerning Psalm 139: "I Love this psalm; it's a beautiful picture of God's intimate knowledge of us." He concluded, "Verse five is probably my favorite because it really paints a picture of one being sealed and protected by God."

The Scriptures state much concerning the stage of development and framing Love. We are taught that children are a heritage of the Lord (see Psalm 127:3). Child rearing is crucial in determining the future of the next generation. Discipline is an act of parental Love. And Jesus showed this as He defended the children who were brought to Him. This shows that there can be no doubt that it is God's will that we grow and experience the intricate processes of development and framing Love. As this world becomes more chaotic, our children become more exposed to the conflicts of violence, to child abuse, and to the conflict between their parents. It is therefore incumbent on all Christian leaders to express and teach this generation how to be emotionally connected to one another in Love.

We are certain that our stage of development represents God's perfect will for our lives. Psalm 139 clearly expresses God's intimate relationship and His continued Love for His people. For this reason everyone is encouraged to study this psalm that they may gain a broader knowledge of how intricately God has created us. Framing Love expresses the heart of God in a special and particular way so that we can feel and enjoy special loving bond between us and our loving Father.

WALK THROUGH

Oh Jesus!

I want the world to know who You are and to believe that You reign supreme forever. Father, you are the only true God. Thank You for imparting within me Your purpose, Your good will and Your fundamental truth. Even though I complain as You guide me through the different processes, I thank You, Lord for being so patient and forgiving! Lord I do recognize how complete a masterpiece I am. I have been transformed into a different person who is now endowed with the mind of Christ. I desire to be completely free from sin and to complete become the righteous of God through Christ Jesus our Lord. I am in Your Kingdom, because I am moving forward to the place that You have prepared for me. What is in this for me? Eternal life—a breakthrough from mortal to immortality!

My salvation lies in Your Word. My vow is to serve You, and to remain with You forever; thank You Lord for allowing room in your heart for me. I am grateful for time I spend in your presence; it empowers me with the feeling of security and confidence.

Don't matter where you serve in His barn, God Loves you – because you are living a life like Christ's.

—Merits Henry

"…ask for the ancient paths, Where the good way is, and walk in it; And you will find rest for your souls. But they said, 'We will not walk in it.'"

—Jeremiah 6:16 (NASB)

CHAPTER SIX

First Love In God

*T*he 'First Love' experience is being at a higher Love and depth in fellowship with the Lord. It also brings on a life-transforming experience which changes our character and everything about us and about who we really are. That experience also sows seeds of goodwill into our hearts that later transform our life into a life of new beginning. First Love helps us to develop that unquenchable desire to be Christ-like. It comes with the passion for spiritual things.

First Love is used simultaneously and interchangeably in Revelation 2:4 and Jeremiah 6:16. This referred to God's perfect will as it relates to our spiritual covenant with Him. Nothing can compare to the Love of God. God's Love is the Love that brings salvation to a dying world. 'The Love of God is greater far than pen or tongue can ever tell.' It cannot be measured neither can it be compared.

Sometimes, the term 'First Love' may not be easily defined. Nevertheless, it can be effortlessly experienced. Once we have experienced the Love of God, it becomes our spiritual dictate. The psalmist David, in one of his psalms (Psalm 51), lamented in repentance to God, because he had often strayed from the will of God. David prayed to the Lord, asking Him to: *"Restore unto me the joy of thy salvation; and uphold me with thy free spirit"* (Psalm 51:12, KJV).

Even though David was the King of Israel, each time that he found himself straying away from the will of the Lord, he would repent and seek to get back to that place of intimacy with the Lord. It is no wonder then that the Lord refers to David 'as a man of His own heart'. First Love draws those who seek after the Lord toward the spiritual things of God and helps them to focus on repairing their broken relationships, and their lives with the Lord.

Love commands that we must be with those whom we care about (Song of Solomon 2). Nothing successful in life is a request, rather it is a desire. This explains the importance of First Love to us. The Love of God is given:

> *for our inspiration and it is profitable for doctrine, for reproof, for correction, and for instruction in righteousness: That the man of God may be made perfect, thoroughly furnished unto all good works.*
> —2 Timothy 3:16–17, KJV

This gives us a glimpse of how fulfilled one can become when one is embraced by the Love of God. This takes us back to the old landmark of Jeremiah 6:16. First Love brings conviction, conversion, correction, and it also brings us cleansing and comfort. First Love is completely above and beyond anything that we could ever experience; First Love is the first step in the rebuilding of our relationship with God. It is the landmark between the Lord and His people (Jeremiah 6:16–17, Proverbs 22:28).

At our conversion, First Love places within us a thirst and a hunger for greater things. There is nothing more satisfying to the human soul than to experience the true and blessed Love of God (Revelation 2). This should inspire us to walk in the righteousness and in the blessedness of the Lord, following in the footsteps of our First Love.

Nothing should keep us from the house of the Lord when we take our first step to salvation. It will change our lives forever and keep us as we press forward, even in the midst of disappointment. Salvation is God working in us, wherever we go. As such, it creates the desires within us, enabling us to have fellowship with one another; showing Love, kindness, honor and respect to all men.

First Love is the gift and the calling of the church, as revealed from the Heart of God. It is a constant flow of power within us. When life is just about us only and not others, the message we present is a message of discord (see Luke 22:24–30). In the book of Revelation, the people left their First Love, but it was the spirit of the Lord that brought them new hope in the Lord. We forgot, and we may tend to give up, at times, but God's First Love never dies. First Love reveals the heart of God, and is a promise covenant that will never be forgotten by the Lord. Therefore, when we surrender to the will of the Lord, He will reignite our First Love back to life. As revealed in His Word, "There are many devices in a man's heart; nevertheless the counsel of the Lord, that shall stand" (Proverbs 19:21, KJV).

A seed does not die but always reproducing more seedlings to replenish that which had been sown. So, therefore, you must always be prepared for your divinely inspired First Love in order that you may be rewarded with your new spiritual gifts. Our First Love is the continuous covenant that we had we made with the Lord. It cannot die, as the Scripture divinely states, "...*I shall not die but I shall live and declare the works of the Lord*" (Psalm 118:17, KJV).

When we are willing to carry the Lord's message of First Love, God will honor His word above His name, as promised, that with long life and prosperity will He reward us. Therefore, we should never be disconnected, from the purpose for which we were born. It is in such time we prevail, when we surrender and reconcile with the Lord, our First Love. That is the time when we should refocus and become quickened again with the Love of God.

Let us not consider sacrificing our First Love, which is the Love of God, for such Love is God in us. Just as First Love is the holy desire of God for us, so then, Satan is the counterfeit of that First Love. Remember it was Satan's desire to have Peter, but God prayed for him, encouraging him that: "*Thy faith fail not: and when thou art converted, strengthen thy brethren*" (Luke 22:32, KJV).

Peter was walking with God, but in ignorance he yielded to Satan's vices as he became fearful. As the enemy worked on Peter's fear, Jesus prayed for him, encouraging him to be strong. This is understandable when we are not vigilant in walking with our 'First Love.'

When Jesus used the phrase, "When thou art converted," in the original Greek, it conveys the meaning, "When you retrace your steps."[16] In other terms, it can be likened to a hunter retracing the footprints of a deer for supper. The standard solution of Jesus' saying this would be for Peter to research his 'ground back' or 'old land mark' and even his 'heritage' to his First Love. How is this possible? Jesus was always conscious of Peter's

---

16 Darlene Bishop, The Transforming Power of Spiritual Desire (Denver: Legacy Publishers Int., 2005), 32.

weakness, therefore He wanted Peter to be in the process of retracing his identity, to protect himself from becoming a prey to the evil one. First Love is always aware of our sinful nature, and of our slavery to sin, before it is revealed to us in signs of dreams, visions, prophecy or songs. Nonetheless, First Love will reawaken our spiritual desires. We can always depend on God's First Love for our protection.

It was only after Peter had retraced his steps that he was personally convicted concerning the truth, and only then was he able to strengthen his brothers. God sometimes allow certain events in our lives to teach us, so that we may experience the light of God's Love and His grace. Peter was uncertain of his situation, but after Jesus had died and risen from the dead, Peter understood, and discovered that everything Jesus had said to him was the truth. (See Mark 14:66–72, Luke 22:60–62.) But Peter said:

> *"Man, I do not know what you are talking about." Immediately, while he was still speaking, a rooster crowed. The Lord turned and looked at Peter. And Peter remembered the word of the Lord, how He had told him, "Before a rooster crows today, you will deny me three times." And he went out and wept bitterly.*
> —Luke 22:60–62, NASB

You see, First Love does not leave us behind; but it reminds us of our past, and shows us our future. It is by acknowledging who we are that we will be able to understand our future. It is time that each one of us retraced our steps, thus allowing our spiritual life to flourish.

Peter was converted to his First Love; he was restored, then he was able to strengthen his brothers. Has God not restored us more than once? He is faithful and will do it again. After all, He is *"the same yesterday, today and forever"* (Hebrews 13:8, NIV). Yes, He will restore us again. The power of First Love brings genuine results and life changing experiences (Act 3, John 9:1–12 and Mark 8:23–25). That is the beauty of First Love!

Satan saw the potential in Peter as he set about to deceive him, but Jesus prayed that his faith would not fail. First Love reveals God's desires for us and shows us the future and the vision of our lives.

WALK THROUGH

Please Lord,

Teach me how to live and practice Your Love to everyone–not today only, Lord, but always. Thank You, Lord, for being my friend and my guide. You have been watching over me, so that I will not go astray. My desire, Lord, is that You will fulfill the plan You have for me.

Lord are you so kind, compassionate and understanding. I know that as of now, I will continue to walk with You. I will worship You with fear and trembling, so as to secure my faith in You, as You prepare for me a place in Heaven where I will reign with You some day.

Truly You desire complete surrender. Thank You for showing me the path to Your grace, dear Lord.

Amen.

SUMMARY AND REFLECTION

Complete the following:

1. Stage development is governed by _____ and shows how effective the process of growing progressively and in Love is.

2. Framing Love reveals the signature of the heart and includes the elements of _____, _____ and _____.

3. Framing Love _____ us with the benefits of God.

4. By definition, First Love is _____.

5. Once we experience God's First Love, it becomes part of our _____ detector.

6. Love reveals the purpose of God's _____ in us.

7. We are not complete until we have _____ Love and
_____.

True or False?

8. God does not have great plans for our lives. _____.
9. First Love is not a request, it is a desire. _____.
10. Every success in life is a desire. _____.

EVALUATION AND TEMPERAMENT

1. How would you rate your experience with the Lord?

   a) Very intimate, personal and rewarding
   b) Moderate
   c) On and off
   d) Poor
   e) No relationship at all.

2. Write down three feelings that you learn from reading Framing Love:

   a) _____
   b) _____
   c) _____

3. On the scale of 1 – 5, with 5 being the highest, what would be your balanced score of the change First Love brought in you _____

   a) No change at all.
   b) Slightly different changes from the old Adamic nature.
   c) Average changes (Lukewarm experience).
   d) More godly changes (e.g. conviction, cleansing, comfort and Love).
   e) Total life changing and reviving experiences.

4. Write down three things that you keep complaining about.

   a) _____
   b) _____

c) _____

5. Write down some of your goals to obtain a relationship with God, your spouse and others as you are convicted by reading Framing Love.

    a) _____
    b) _____
    c) _____
    d) _____

6. Complete: After reading Framing Love and First Love in God, I realized that:

_____

_____

_____

_____

Love Request

Things that are missing from your life and that you would like to experience to be at peace with yourself and most importantly with Jesus in relation to the lesson. It is challenging to express Love and to excel in kindness according to the word of God.

"Thus says the Lord of hosts, Render true judgments, show kindness and mercy to one another" (Zechariah 7:9, ESV).

"Search me, God, and know my heart...." (Psalm 139:23, NIV).

Write down three words of supplication that you would like to see manifested, reaffirmed and resolved in your life, family and friendships.

_____

_____

_____

PART TWO

Love Sees With New Eyes

"Brethren, if anyone is caught in any transgression,
you who are spiritual should restore him in a spirit of gentleness.
Keep watch over yourself,
lest you too be tempted."

—Galatians 6:1, ESV

Growing From Your Mistakes

The Love of God allows us to see ourselves in the beauty of holiness, and it also allows us to become more appreciative of the blessedness of Christ Jesus. The Love of God renews the mind; it mends the broken heart and it also brings peace and joy to those who are lonely. God's Love allows us to be free from fear and to be at peace with those around us.

As David states: *"Make me to hear joy and gladness; that the bones which thou hast broken may rejoice"* (Psalm 51:6, KJV). Love gives you that assurance that you are forgiven, that you are important, and that you are worthy of the Love of God.

Isaiah states that: *"Instead of your shame you shall have double honor… Everlasting joy shall be theirs"*(Isaiah 61:7, NKJV).

Love allows a second chance; Love looks beyond the faults of others; Love is merciful and is ready to forgive. Love is also willing to restore the joy of salvation to those who had lost their joy (1 Corinthians 13). Love sees us as lilies among the thorns, and also as the beautiful Rose of Sharon, even in our failures.

At times we are overly anxious to experience the presence of God in our lives. However, like the seeds in the farmers' field, we do experience change. But, in the midst of our expectation there is the virtue of time that comes through the ray of hope to challenge our trust, and to make us want to give up. Nevertheless, this is when we must wait on the Lord–that is the time when we should put our faith and our trust in the Lord. There is always someone whom the Lord will use to bring His Love through to you, someone who certainly will not turn you away. You must keep on believing. "Faith moments are miracle moments" (Mike Murdock).

The miracle at Zarephath that took place between Elijah and the widow is an example of the ability to recognize and follow the voice of the Lord. The widow had every reason to question Elijah's words, but she did not question him. Instead she believed him because she had something that not everyone in her situation had; she had the ability to discern the truth in faith and not in self-pity. She could have decided to eat her last meal and die as she had stated, but instead she obeyed the voice of the Lord by believing what the man of God told her. Her faith was tempered with Love. She was a woman of great faith, a faith that she used to unlock the miracles of God (1King 17:7-16).

The Lord Loves us so much that He will always send someone in our lives to unlock our faith, but we must be able to acknowledge the moment of our miracle. As we help others, even when we are broken, even when it appears that all hope is lost, the Lord, in His Love and mercy for us, releases favors in our lives. God, in His mercy, is ever pursuing us with Love. Even in our faults, the heart of the Lord is ever open to receive us. But are you ready to receive the Love of God?! All that the Lord needs of us is that we keep His commandments.

We must remember that even though we may have grown in the Lord, and have reached a state of maturity in Him, it is still very important that we as believers, "...be stedfast, unmovable" (1 Corinthian 15:58) in the Love of Jesus. We must always seek to abound in the grace of God. Nevertheless, the principle of growth is required at every stage of our new growth. For example, when the Lord spoke with Jeremiah, saying, "...Like the clay in the pot maker's hand, so are you in my hand..." (Jeremiah 18:6, NLV). We must then recognize that God is the potter and we are the clay as He molds us, as He breaks us and as He refashions us into His own image and into His own likeness.

The Lord chastens those whom He loves by disciplining them with compassion and with wisdom.) The Word of God states you are God's workmanship. According to Christian Psychology and Counseling, Dr. Roger and his professors said, "The bottom line of positive and stable self-esteem is when you can say: 'I accept the value that God has put on me, when you do that you will then cooperate with God to develop the best possible you in this world.'"

Our desire for the things of the Lord must be more important than our desire for the things of this world. Paul instructed the believers to: "*Set your affection on the things above, not on things on the earth*" (Colossians 3:2, KJV).

We should encourage those who are successful in the things of this world to set their desire not on their achievements, but on the hope and promises of God, as well as not ignoring their own limitations, and understanding that the Lord is the source of all their earthly achievements.

One can decide to be a winner if one chooses to learn from his past success, or one can decide to be a loser if one chooses to listen to the voice of failure. Our true faith is to be assured of what we hope for and to be ready to receive the things that we cannot see. Through all our mistakes God is teaching us to have faith in Him. The desire of the Lord is for us to be winners in everything we do; but we must be committed to the things of the Lord by keeping His commandments.

The law of sowing and reaping guarantees that we will reap the rewards of the choices and the decisions we make. But through the grace of the Lord, and through His Love towards us, we are assured that because of His faithfulness we are confident that He is there all the time with His outstretched arms, waiting to receive us.

WALK THROUGH

Most Holy God! The creator of this world, the giver of lives, the infallible and unchanged lover of my soul, I thank You. I thank You for Your unmerited grace that You have bestowed on my life this day. As I present the different specific requests, please help me to grow in grace, so that I may make the right decisions. Lord, I want my life to be Christ-motivated by Your perfect will. I desire Your will to define who and for whom I am and not what I wish for myself to be. Please Lord! Help me in every stage of my life to sow the right seeds, so that I can reap the harvest that You have ordained for my life.

Last but not least, dear Lord, help me to grow from every mistake. The reason I desire this request, is because I want my life to be a sum total of transformation to my associates. You are my living source of purpose, and I recognize Your work in my life. Give me this day, enough faith to believe with You that this shall be and that such mistakes will never happen again.

Thank You, Jesus!

Leading By Loving, The Called To Be Leaders Of His People

Christian leaders face many difficult challenges as they assume the highest office and the responsibilities that come with it, as they lead and minister to the children of the Lord. There are three very crucial modes of preparation which the Christian leaders must be willing to go through once they have recognized and have accepted that they have been called, by the Lord, to lead His people to salvation:

1. The forsaking of the things of this world; they are expected to live up to a higher standards, and to greater expectations, according to the Scriptures, and not according to the standards of the expectations of the world;

2. The heart of a Christian leader must be transformed by the instructions of the Holy Spirit, as the fruit of the Spirit must be visibly shown through their leadership;

3. The Christian leader must be willing to stand, with boldness and for righteousness sake; with valor, he must stand for the righteousness of the Lord, regardless of earthly situations; he must boldly stand for God.

The desire to lead the people of God demands a higher standard by such leaders than from those who had not really been called by the Lord to lead His people into righteousness. It is also a covenant that Christian leaders jointly make with the Lord when they assume the responsibility of leadership role in the Kingdom of God. The expectation is great, the responsibility is demanding and the covenant is everlasting. The Lord will never break His covenant, but those who assume leadership position in the Kingdom of the Lord and break the joint covenant that they had made with Him, will receive their reward of everlasting punishment. The Scripture declares: "*Woe to the pastors who are scattering and destroying the sheep of my pasture…*" (Jeremiah 23:1, NASB).

The heart of a Christian leader must be transformed by the renewing of the Holy Spirit, and by the transformation of His human nature through the studying of the Word of God. The desire to become leaders of God's people cannot be motivated by the zeal to climb the ladder of success so that one might become great in the eyes of men, but it must be a response to the call of the Lord, to prepare His people whom the Lord has entrusted into the spiritual care and nurturing of spiritual leaders. This position of leadership is not a position for earthly gain, neither is it a position that will attract the accolades of the world, but it is a position that is heavenly ordained. It is a position that comes with divine accolades when the Lord will say, "*Well done, my good and faithful servant...*" (Matthew 25: 23, NLT).

Remember Jesus in His ministry on earth never sought after the things of this world. He never accepted an invitation to sit at the tables of kings, or at the tables of governors, neither did He eat at the homes of any of the rich Jewish leaders of His day. No, Jesus never rode in chariots, neither did He ride on the backs of the Roman military horses, but during His ministry on earth, He sought shelter in the humblest of abodes and ate at the tables of tax collectors.

Jesus had no mansions of His own; He had nowhere to lay His head, but He knew and understood that His divine mission on earth was to redeem mankind back unto His Father. Jesus visited those with whom the society of His day had rejected. Yes, instead of riding in chariots, He rode on the back of the humblest of beasts—He rode on the back of a donkey. Jesus, who was the Word that became flesh, came and lived among us and rejected the demands of Satan when he tempted Him by asking that Jesus should fall down and worship him for the riches of this world. Jesus gave up His throne in heaven so that He could redeem mankind back unto His father. Christian leaders, those are the expectations that are demanded of you from the Lord. Anything less than having the characteristics of Jesus

Christ, as Christian leaders, constitutes the breaking of the covenant agreement between you and the Lord. As with Jesus, the Lord also demands the same leadership qualities from those to whom He would entrust with the leadership of His people.

The Lord knows and sees what no one else can discern–He knows and sees leadership qualities in those whom He calls to lead. Jephthah, the ninth judge of Israel was a mighty man of valor, even though he began his life as the son of a prostitute (Judges 11:1). Yet the plan of God for his life was for him to be the next leader of Israel. Many are the plans of man but it is the plan of the Lord that will prevail (Proverbs 19:21). Jephthah was rejected and dishonored by his own family because he was born of another woman. No inheritance was given to him, and he had to leave the country where he was born to abide in another country. Imagine the excruciating pain and the agony that he must have experienced, being rejected by his own family. The thoughts of committing suicide could have been one of the decisions he was faced with, but God, in His mercy, delivered him. The thought of taking revenge on his brothers could have entered his mind; but God's plans for his life had defeated the voice of discouragement, and led him into a life of accomplishment. Through His Love and His plan for our lives, the Lord will use even the base things of this world to accomplish His purpose.

Our God always makes a way when there seems to be no way out of situations. God allowed the Ammonites to come up against Israel in battle. Israel was terrified because of the threats of the Ammonites to capture their land and they had no one to turn to for help. They thought that they had no leader, but the Lord, through His infallible power and mercy and through His Love for the children of Israel, looked through eternity and saw a man who would defend His people. Jephthah was a mighty man of valor and Israel needed a mighty warrior, one who had no fear of facing the enemy. Even with the guilt of their past memories, and even with their conscience bothering them, they requested the help of the one whom they had rejected and expelled from their land; they called on the warrior, Jephthah. Man will expel us but God is our righteous judge. The Word of the Lord declares that: "...*the stone that the builders rejected has become the cornerstone*" (Psalm 118:22, ESV). Through His Love, and through His mercies, the Lord allows: "...*all things to work together for good to those who love God*" (Romans 8:28, NASB).

It is God who determines who will be favored in His Kingdom. One should not worry concerning the thoughts of others, but the focus should be on the plan of God for one's life. Jephthah became their leader. 'Love reveals the heart of God.'

WALK THROUGH

Dear Lord Jesus:

I thank You for choosing me. I did not understand what the true purpose for my life was, neither could I have understood my own weaknesses. However, after I had given my life over to You, the identity of who You had determined me to be, revealed who I am and what my purpose is, according to Your will for me on earth.

Today, I am serving in your harvest field with Love, by helping others to see their true purpose in You, dear Jesus.

Amen.

"… full of joy through the Holy Spirit, [Jesus] said, "I praise you, Father, Lord of heaven and earth, because you have hidden these things from the wise and learned, and revealed them to little children. Yes, Father, for this is what you were pleased to do."

—Luke 10:21 NIV

About Your Heart In His Heart

What was the thought of our Lord when He created us? No one knows the heart of the Lord. But one thing we do know is that we were marvelously designed and divinely fashioned by the gracious hands of God, who then poured His everlasting Love within our hearts and afterwards proclaimed the marvelous work of His own hands. There is nothing that can be compared with the Love of God, towards mankind. The Lord lovingly created us in His own image, and breathed His own life-giving spirit within us, thus making us into His own likeness, and into His own reflection on earth. Mankind was lovingly created by God, to be the heartbeat of the Lord on earth.

Great moments are created when great opportunities are presented. Nevertheless, no other gift could have provided the satisfaction that the human soul desires, except the everlasting gift of the Love of the Lord Jesus who died to redeem the souls of mankind back unto Himself. For this reason, the gift of redemption could only be achieved through the shed blood of the Lord. Now, the Lord, through the provision of His Son, has given us the assurance of the satisfaction of life eternal. Therefore, there is no other gift that can be compared to the everlasting Love of God.

Jesus Christ, on the cross, revealed His compassion and Love toward us, when He was nailed between two thieves. He not only offered His Love to them, but as God, He also offered to them salvation; however, only one of them believed and accepted life everlasting. This further shows that many will not receive Christ, but for those who do receive Him, unto them He will give life eternal. This however, requires acceptance of forgiveness, as demonstrated by the thief on the cross, when he repented of his sins and was immediately welcomed to be with the Lord Jesus in paradise.

Before we can discover the meaning of true Love, we must encourage ourselves in the Lord. Jesus in His faithfulness, before His ascension to heaven, reassured His disciples that He would send the Comforter, which is the Holy Spirit to comfort them during their time of grief; in this they were encouraged. This revelation of emotional attachment that the Lord had with His disciples reveals and demonstrates a higher sense of giving and receiving of genuine Love. It also reveals the positive effect that Love, when demonstrated from the heart, can have on the mind of those who mourn.

Love Is The Hand Of God At Work

The birth of Tamar's twins recorded in Genesis 38 presents an account of God's hand of Love at work, in the heartfelt desire of those who need Love and for the purpose of which Love is intended.

Tamar, a woman who sought justice through deception, by human standards, became justified in her action through the Love of God. Because, through His Love, the Lord justified her action by demonstrating the deception of Judah, and in the process, Tamar in the midst of human deception, brought forth twins, one of whom is listed in the 'genealogy of our Lord Jesus' (Genesis 38: 27–30).

This demonstration shows that the Love of God transcends the understanding of the human mind. And as the Love of God had overshadowed Tamar's twins at birth, and in the process, used them to confuse human understanding, so then, He will also do the same thing for those who believe in Him. If we are faithful and just in our dealings with the things of the Lord, and even when everything appears to be impossible, then we should only remain faithful to Him, by demonstrating our Love to those who are in need of our Love and of our understanding. Tamar had done the only thing she knew to do, so that she could receive the Love and attention she so desired. Love is one of the Lord's ways of revealing His truth to His people, even when we, as His children do not deserve such Love.

As declared by Christ Jesus, through the Apostle Paul in 1 Corinthians 1:18–28, these verses show one of the Lord's ways of revealing His genuine truth wrapped up in Love, as God's power and wisdom. This defect is not a human conclusion, but is a spontaneous supernatural power, an inspiration colored with the symbols denoting the existence of God that changes hell, heaven and humanity. The manifold wisdom of God by Paul's revelation of these inspired thoughts is recorded below:

> *For the message of the cross is foolishness to those who are perishing, but to us who are being saved it is the power of God.*
>
> *For it is written: I will destroy the wisdom of the wise; the intelligence of the intelligence I will frustrate.*
>
> *Where is the wise person? Where is the teacher of the law? Where is the philosopher of this age? Has not God made foolish the wisdom of the world?*
>
> *For since in the wisdom of God the world through its wisdom did not know him, God was pleased through the foolishness of what was preached to save those who believed.*
>
> *Jews demand signs and Greeks look for wisdom, but we preach Christ crucified: a stumbling block to Jews and foolishness to Gentiles, but to those whom God has called, both Jews and Greeks, Christ the power of God and the wisdom of God. For the foolishness of God is wiser than human wisdom, and the weakness of God is stronger than human strength.*
>
> *Brothers and sisters, think of what you were when you were called. Not many of you were wise by human standards; not many were influential; not many were of noble birth. But God chose the foolish things of the world to shame the wise; God chose the weak things of the world to shame the strong.*
>
> *God chose the lowly things of this world and the despised things—and the things that are not—to nullify the things that are, so that no one may boast before him.*
>
> *It is because of him that you are in Christ Jesus, who has become for us wisdom from God—that is, our righteousness, holiness and redemption. Therefore, as it is written: "Let the one who boasts boast in the Lord."*
>
> —1 Corinthians 1:18–31, NIV

Through the manifold wisdom of God, He has chosen some from birth, some to be leaders and some to be the heirs of wealth, while others are chosen to be the remnant of purpose to their family, while others are chosen to be the standard bearers of light to others "….*because God has chosen you from the beginning for salvation through sanctification by the Spirit and faith in the truth,*" (2 Thessalonians 2:13, NASB) "*…and the LORD hath chosen thee to be a peculiar people unto himself, above all the nations that [are] upon the earth*" (Deuteronomy 14:2, KJV), and also, "*… I formed thee in the belly, I knew thee; and before thou camest forth out of the womb I sanctified thee, and I ordained thee a prophet unto the nations*" (Jeremiah 1:5, KJV). As stated in Genesis 17:19–21, God gave His covenant to Isaac and not to Ishmael, even though Ishmael was the first born son of Abraham, because Ishmael's birth came as a result of his parents' choosing. However, the birth of Isaac was ordained from the beginning (a typology of grace) when the Lord declared to His parents that they would bring forth a son. This indicates to us that this covenant was a covenant of First Love, but we, as human beings have failed to understand that the Word of the Lord stands supreme, regardless of the decisions we, as believers, want to make.

There is no question that the Lord would have chosen Isaac, the promised son, over Ishmael. Broken covenants with the Lord cause confusion and therefore bring desolation to those who have broken the Lord's covenant. Even though Ishmael was blessed by the Lord, the covenant of promise from generation to generation was with Isaac.

Isaac had twin sons, Esau and Jacob, and the Lord appointed the older to serve the younger (Genesis 25: 23). This is an example of how the Lord in His unique way invokes His blessing on whomever He chooses. The story of each set of twins in the Bible points to an official ceremony of blessings against greed, jealousy, hatred, or because of the displeasure of the Lord against their parents. The references that have been made have revealed the awesomeness of the Lord, and that he, as God, chooses to show His power and His Love through whom He will. Only when we as mankind can understand the awesomeness of our Lord will we be able to come to the knowledge and understanding of His Love.

The Love of God is a transforming force that delights the heart of man. Through this Love, it is the desire of the Lord to grant us the true desires of our hearts. This promise should inspire us to keep the Lord's commandments and to attain for higher heights in the Lord. This will, through His grace, make all the difference as we aim for higher heights and deeper depths in the things of the Lord.

By the law and custom of inheritance of ancient time, the inheritance normally belonged to the firstborn. This act was interesting on the path of Rachael's and Tamar's servants. The firstborn is normally chosen to inherit the blessings and the inheritance of their father, without exception. But God, in His divine will, sees things differently through His purpose, through His desire and through His Love. Using our human knowledge, we may use our 'common sense' to define the parents' distribution of their wealth to their children, but God in mercy sees beyond our human understanding, and even before conception, He already knows the thoughts of the human heart, as He declared unto Jeremiah, *"...before I formed you in the womb, I knew you"* (Jeremiah 1:5, ESV). The thoughts of the Lord are beyond human understanding, therefore, we as human beings, have no choice but to believe and accept the doings of the Lord as He bestows His Love upon those whom He chooses, as only He alone knows the heart of man.

Love sees with new eyes as it looks into the future without being astonished (Proverbs 29:18; Philippians 1:6, 7; 1Samuel 16:7; Luke 16: 15; John 8:15.) As Love listens, it wisely changes human's preference and gives first privilege to the unexpected. Divine Love sees beyond the normal. It will look into the future first, and then, it will reverse the privileges. Pharez, through God's Love, had a messianic breakthrough, and as a result, the foundation on which Christ, the Messiah was born came through the seed of a woman. On this the church stands as a rock and as beacon of light for our salvation and our stronghold, against which the gates of hell were manifested. According to the Scripture, before Tamar had given birth to Pharez and his brother Zarah, on the way out, Zarah was forced out of the way by his brother Pharez, who should have been the last to arrive, but instead, he became the first-born. Hence it is said of Pharez: *"What a breach you have made for yourself!"* (Genesis 38:29, ESV). It is worth noting that human knowledge will never be able to understand the power of the Lord's doings. Zarah's hand might have been the first to appear, but all things are ordained according to purpose of the Lord.

It does not mean that a breakthrough that has been delayed for many years will not eventually come through, but it will only be according to the divine will of the Lord. God's favor is on everyone who keeps His commandments. However, as His children, the Lord sees us completely differently from the way the world sees us because we are His chosen.

With the birth of Tamar's twins, the midwife clearly expected the child on whose hand she placed the thread to be the firstborn, the firstborn as defined by her cultural understanding. By marking the child's hand with a scarlet thread, the midwife sensed that something miraculous was about to take place. As the mother, Tamar also knew that her second child, the one that came first, was the divine plan of the Lord and that the child was chosen to be great in the Kingdom of God. The chain of bondage was broken, beginning with the birth of Tamar's twins as an example of God's plan for redemption. As noted in 1 Corinthians 15: "So it is written: "The first man Adam became a living being"; the last Adam, a life-giving spirit" (1 Corinthians 15:45, NIV)."

Through this combination of prophecies, we discover the exceptional wisdom of God's design. Through God's Love for His people, the chain of bondage was broken with the second Adam. Jesus, the first fruit of them that slept (see 1 Corinthians 15:20) and the first to be resurrected from the dead, in so doing, defeated death by taking the keys of death and hell. He is now seated at the Father's right hand, making intercession for our redemption.

According to Revelation 20:1, a triumphant proclamation was declared by Jesus unto us—his Church! *"I am the Living One; I was dead, and now look, I am alive for ever and ever! And I hold the keys of death and Hades"* (Revelations 20:1, NIV).

Given another inspiration, Paul also speaks of God's unmerited affirmation as: *"... Christ Jesus is the one who died—more than that, who was raised—who is at the right hand of God, who indeed is interceding for us"* (Romans 8:34, ESV).

The midwife could have manipulated Zarah's body by using her hand but she remembered that vigilance is the price of safety. As Zarah withdrew his hand, behold his brother came forth (Genesis 38:29). God's purpose must be fulfilled, regardless of man's desire. Nothing or anyone cannot alter the destiny of those whom the Lord has chosen to perform His will on earth, as, *"For whom he did foreknow, he also did predestinate to be conformed to the image of His Son, that he might be the firstborn among many brethren"* (Romans 8:29, KJV). Pharez became the firstborn because the plan of the enemy could not have overridden the divine plan of God. The midwife's response to Pharez having "broken through" is an indication that she was surprised at the situation with which she was confronted. She questioned as to how this could have happened, allowing for the change in circumstances for these babies to be born. In like manner to Jesus' situation and the battle He had with Satan, after He was crucified, buried and resurrected, it became apparent that Satan was deceived by Christ's resurrection, as Jesus triumphantly emerged as the savior of the world.

When vision is seen, purpose is born. When Love is given, our assignment becomes God's involvement. As in the case of the midwife, her purpose was not to benefit Tamar's assignment by assisting her with giving birth to twins but by God's divine plan, she was strategically appointed to stay there until her assignment was completed. Staying there meant that the assignment was not completed, and above all, only the discerning could have recognized this greatness. Our assignment has a time and a process likewise. Thus, we should not panic if it is taking a while, but instead we should stay there, as the Scripture declares in Isaiah 40:31:

> *But they that wait upon the Lord shall renew their strength; they shall mount up with wings as eagles; they shall run, and not be weary; and they shall walk, and not faint.*
> —Isaiah 40:31, KJV

Tamar had two babies, Pharez and Zarah, but in Pharez was Judah, that is Salvation. The name Pharez is translated to mean, the 'Rock, which came from the Aramaic Language, the language spoken by Jesus, which is Petros in Greek. It was after the birth of Pharez that the midwife was able to assist Zarah into a better position for his safe delivery. Without the guidance of the Lord, we would have had no power to perform the tasks that He has assigned to us.

God has fulfilled His Love through the justification of Pharez's birth, and by His wondrous work, through the birth of Jesus, two thousand years ago, which will continue even unto the end of this present world. We are the divine work of the Lord, showing forth His everlasting light in this world, thus fulfilling His everlasting covenant that He made with mankind.

"Oh Lord, how great are thy works!" (Psalm 92:5, KJV) The midwife clearly had experienced the divine power of God through the birth of Tamar's twins. Truly, God, as He had protected Pharez, so too had He protected us in our mother's womb, as He worked out His purpose for our life. Surely He has seen us through the eyes of Love, beholding His

beauty within us; seeing us as His wonderful creation, as He declared that we are *"fearfully and wonderfully made"* (Psalm 139:14, NIV). The Scripture again declares, that: *"Christ in you, the hope of glory"* (Colossians 1:27, KJV). As with Tamar and her twins, God certainly will do, and He always does wondrous things to protect His chosen people. What peace and what Love it brings us to know that there is a Savior who will fulfill our desires when we place our trust in Him. It is in Him we live and it is in Him we have our being. By His loving arms He protects us, with His loving eyes, He watches over us, and through His divine power, a miracle is performed in our lives every day. But we must be persuaded by the 'word,' that God is Love.

THROUGH THE LOVE OF GOD, MIRACLES ARE PERFOMED EVERY DAY

There is a break-through in our lives when the Love of God is shining through us. However, God must be first in our lives, if we must achieve that breakthrough

We are first by God's design. Therefore, there is no option of us being second being a quitter in God's design ordained by Jesus. Therefore, we are God's first class and God's gateway to greater success. We are His front-line object wrapped in purpose, as opposed to the subject of failure. Even though Zarah's hand first came out, it was ordained according to purpose with divine assignment to have Pharez be the first. Isn't it motivating when we can encourage ourselves in the Lord, even when others have bullied our confidence? Despite having been broken, cast down or forsaken by others, we can still encourage our soul with the Word of God, as David did in Psalm 42. Instead of believing the lies of the world, we can roll back the curtain of memories now and then. Doing this is one way of looking into the mirror of God's love to overcome such disquieting spirits within.

When one encounters a minute of delay or set back, it is a means for God to work out His purpose in us. Nevertheless, it does not mean that we will not break through. As we wait on the Lord, I can assure you by declaring that every breakthrough that has been delayed for this year will come forth! Yes! It is coming through in less than seconds, minutes, hours, days and weeks. By God's favor being imputed to us, there is as well a scepter of grace being provided. Thus, we are the number one heartbeat within God's Love.

What an awesome God! We cannot live without Him. Because God is Love, and all of His creation must reflect His Love. Yet, we, as His chosen people do not always understand the impact of His blessedness, of His Love and of His anointing power over us. If we should truly understand God's universal Love for us, we would have been more willing to endure the process which would enable us to receive God's free salvation. Also, we would have been better able to endure the cross and bear the shame as Christ had done. One must remember the process through which Tamar's twins were born. Tamar experienced severe grief, but through it all, she endured, thus making it possible for the miracles and the power of the Lord to be fulfilled.

God is giving us a hand, a handshake of Love, which magnetically pulls us to come out into green pastures. May I say this unto us: pursue the dream and don't look back. God's perspective is to move us into a decided vision that will only take one day for Him to fulfill His promises unto us. As stated:

> *For no matter how many promises God has made, they are "Yes" in Christ. And so through him the "Amen" is spoken by us to the glory of God. Now it is God who makes both us and you stand firm in Christ. He anointed us, set his seal of ownership on us, and put his Spirit in our hearts as a deposit, guaranteeing what is to come.*
> —2 Corinthians 1:20-22, NIV

Love delights in the entire adventure of us. Nobody can truly understand the message of our heart, except us. Under the direction of Love, revelation sees abundance. Our natural inclination is to see that the first comes out on top, but in the heart of God's chamber, it is the opposite sometimes. As the word of God profoundly says in Matthew, *"So the last will be first, and the first will be last"* (Matthew 20:16, NIV). This statement of declaration portrays the direction of purpose, achievement and new beginning. Unfortunately, our true colors come out unexpectedly, but they are going nowhere. Needless to say, it happens to all of us. Nevertheless, we must be confident and declare: 'our goal in life is not to be exclusively last.' Our perception of life is to acquire something that is meaningful, is different, and is purposeful.

The Love of Jesus showcases us differently from the world. The world sees us with the silver hardware of human insight but God's Love sees us as pure golden treasures, trapped in clay vessels. Because Love lives in the present and sees the future, it generally attracts vision but the pursuit of human Love surrounds the past and only sees the present. Since Love sees and lives the future, it can be recognized by God's assignment placed within the person. With a loving heart that is born to serve as an incubator for dreams, greatness and vision will continue to the purpose of Christ's coming. That way, when our calling is hidden in rags, it will not die in fear, but will survive in swaddling clothes of Love. According to Myles Munroe, "We are something wrapped in nothing." Ultimately, this is Love, because it takes on nothing to make us into something. Did we deserve to have salvation? No! But Christ's Love does all of that in the process of becoming something wrapped in nothing.

God sees us with a dimension of truth with an intention called Love, God's Love! We are hidden from the eyes of Herod to become the next assignment of Love. This is and has been His internal way of guiding us, and by protecting us from the snares of falling into the web of deception.

Oftentimes, we may express our own excitement about others, but there should be a greater personhood with Love. When loving through leading becomes a style, by engendering respect the old-fashioned way, overcoming negatives within our control, Love will be contagious. And by contrast, real love is genuine love of God. It is responsible, considerate and is always reverent for one other. Effective Love starts here: leading from living and loving by leading. Therefore, any hope of seeing others prevail should be encouraged.

Our names have been written in the eternal book of life from the foundation of the world. God knew us before we were conceived. When we were led astray, and when we had turned away from Him, He was there waiting with an outstretched hands to lift us up again; for through it all, God still Loves us with an everlasting Love.

The Scripture declares that we are one in Christ, meaning that we should all have the mind of Christ. *"I will put my spirit in you"* (Ezekiel 37:14, NIV) says the Lord. When God breathes into us the breath of life it is His Love that He extends to us. The power of Love and the power to Love had been given unto us by the Lord. We may not be able to fully understand the wisdom of God, but if we submit ourselves to His will, He will reveal Himself to us through the power of His Love.

The Love of God is made manifest through us; as He keeps us daily in thoughts (Psalm 68:19). As the Lord declares: *"...for I know the plans I have for you..."* (Jeremiah 29:11, NASB). As it relates to true discernment, the heart of the individual has to be pure if he is to experience the revelation and Love of Jesus Christ. *"Blessed are the pure in heart for they shall see God"* (Matthew 5:8, NIV). Therefore, to express discernment we must have the mind of God, we must be transformed by having a renewed heart, a heart that reflects the mind of Christ (1 Corinthians 2:16). It is understood that true discernment is a reflection of the ability to show forth the Love of Christ. The spirit of the Lord will transform one's life so that it becomes a vessel of honor.

That vessel, when transformed, will experience the peace, the joy and the desire to minister the unconditional Love of God in holiness and not as a ritual. When the Love of God indwells the believer's heart, he becomes a refreshing stream as he shares with the world the peace, the gentleness and the contentment of the divine experience of God's Love. On such principles we become one in Christ through the precious gift of God's divine Love.

WALK THROUGH

Dear Father,

How marvelous is thy Love towards us? With a heart of gratitude we come before You. We thank You for the divine Love that You have bestowed on us. The Love that saturates our hearts with Your peace and with Your joy in exchange for our stubborn will. With faithfulness, we say thank You for Your Grace and Your mercy towards us.

Lord, we thank You for renewing a rightful spirit within us. You knew our ways, yet it pleases You to continue showing us Your mercy. Lord, we pray that You will continue surrounding us with Your Holy Spirit, with Your divine Love, with Your merciful favor and with Your grace and mercy each day of our life. Lord we thank You for Your redeeming Love.

Amen!

MODEL APPROACH FOR ALL SETTINGS

- I will resolve to build a positive relationship with my family, through the grace of the Lord, by loving them, and by nurturing them as it is my duty as a ministering servant of God, with faithful commitments, serving and teaching them the Word of God as their priest, their spiritual leader and as the protector of my home.

- I am spiritually responsible for the training and for the up bringing of my children as the Lord had intended me to do, by playing an active role in their lives; I will take responsibility for the task of being the spiritual leader of my family.

- I endeavor to be an example to my family by being a positive influence and role model in their lives, by praying for them and with them. I will encourage and counsel them on how to be successful in their personal endeavors. I will also teach them the fear and admonition of the Lord.

- I will embrace my family, unconditionally as Christ has embraced me. I will uphold the blessedness of my holy matrimony as ordained by the Lord; showing Love and respect, and being understanding and supportive of my partner and by upholding the integrity of our relationship as the Bride of Christ required of us.

- I will always embrace the spirit of reconciliation, knowing that it is God who works through the Holy Spirit, to remind us concerning the examples of forgiveness, through the unity of the Holy Spirit. This is what, as Christian leaders, we are charged to do.

- I want always to demonstrate the Love of God to my family, to my brethren and to the world.

- Reconciliation means that I will humbly acknowledge any unhealthy relationships that I might have had, and be reconciled with those whom I might have hurt.

- The Lord will not allow me to be tempted beyond what I am able to endure, but with the temptation He will provide the way of escape for me, so that I will be able to endure to the end.

- I want to be filled with the divine Love of God, as it is my holy hope, as I encourage others with the Word of God.

- Marriage is a learning process through which one learns to be tolerant, to be devoted, and to be patient.

- In life, I understand that I must be willing to adjust situations to accommodate my spouse and others if I desire to make any progress in my spiritual life.

- A successful marriage does not happen overnight. It resides on the counsel of both parties. My marriage is what you desire it to be.

- Any unconfessed sin, by reasons forbidden in God's Word, can serve as a doorway for the enemy to my life (matrimonially, spiritually, relationally, internally, and personally).

- Nothing can take the place of Love in life, only Christ who is Love. Thus, without Love, I cannot enjoy a successful relationship.

- No life of bliss is therefore totally free from problems. As long as I live in this world and share my life with others, I will experience setbacks.

- Love should be expressed in words and in kind deeds, regardless of the behavior, attitudes, or circumstances of others.

- The Spirit of God who supplies wisdom and Love for effective family relationships and to creatively empower the value system endorsed by the Bible. Furthermore, marriage is not designed to defend the practice of social convenience, unholy pleasure, or to empower the concupiscence of the mind. Its central purpose is to glorify God and to advance His kingdom through a lifelong covenant of marriage which includes God, a man and a woman, to whom the Lord had given the command to be fruitful and multiply.

- A child who is intellectually gifted can be a blessing as well as a source of difficulty in their socialization and emotional growth processes. It is important to bring up a child the way he should go, so that when he is old he will not depart from it.

- Anger should not be one of our main interactions with others.

- Never ignore a child whose desire is to achieve honesty. If you do, this is one factor that may lead to mental illness in children.

- Some children appear to struggle with spiritual and ethical matters, during their different stages of development; for example, right versus wrong. Early divine intervention is crucial at this stage.

- The Scripture is God's message of Love to us. Its words are divinely inspiring, conveying His Love to us. The Scriptures should be read on a daily basis, out of duty and out of commitment.

WORDS OF WISDOM ON LOVE AND ON CHARACTER BUILDING

- Leading by example is a divine way in which one may appeal to one's congregation. It shows an expression of one's belief in the Lord, and should reflect in one's daily life, characterizing the heart and the mind of Christ in such believers.

- Love is not at war with mankind, but it is against the hateful nature of man; it is against the self-centeredness of mankind's behavior toward one another. If Love should declare war with the enemy, how would Love expect to win? Would it not be by pouring the oil of healing where the wounded are held captive?

- Love wages war, not for the destruction of the hateful, but for transforming them over into the truth of God's word.

- It is one of the shepherd's functions to impart the word of knowledge to unbelievers, by pointing them to the true nature of God's Love, and teaching them how the Love of God is used to transform the life of hate into a life of Love

- One must remember that a credential can only get him to an intended position, but it is the Christ-like character that will sustain him in that position. One must always be reminded that it is the heart that will speak always to the issues of the way one lives his life.

- Credentials can easily be rendered unimportant, but it is the person's character that will become a legacy for the next generation to emulate.

- When Love is seen, character develops a legacy, which will leave an impact on the life of others.

- Credentials may incite jealousy and covetousness, but lasting Love will continue to grow into a healthy legacy and into a sincere and lasting relationship.

- Love qualifies our character by reducing the risk of the un known through which it is always prepared to cast its shadow of kindness, over generation to generation to come

- Love is valuable during a time of crisis, because it determines the sincerity of others.

- Beyond this world of pain is a better home where Love dwells, a home filled with such Love that will never fail, but goes unto everlasting and greater glory.

- Love will always value and celebrate the success of others, in the fruit of the spirit.

- Love spends time meditating conditions before crucial decisions are made.

- We do have an intrinsic attribute through which we emulate the loving nature of Christ. Then, as the Love of Christ matures within us, it then enables others to see the Love of God in us as they too come to glorify the Father also.

- Never grow character without understanding Love, because character by itself will become old one day, but through Love, it will never dies. It continues to flourish and replenish, becoming whole.

- We cannot be followers of Christ unless we have the Love of Christ within us. With such a heart of Love, we are made to be Christ-like in our relationships with others, thus demonstrating the attributes and gentleness of God's character.

- Love builds positive character.

- Love connects us with the Lord and this is the intrinsic way we were created to be.

- Now is the time for us to demonstrate our Love to others in our community by becoming concerned and connected with our neighbors' needs.

- Conversion of the heart is the character of God; those who are witnesses to such conversion will yearn to become followers of Christ.

- Genuine Love seizes the opportunity to find confidence in the things of God, and seeks comfort in His mighty arms.

- The followers of God should always be concerned about giving to others and be in the service of others.

- Our godly assignments are sometimes unrecognisable by others because of the lack of understanding and Love. But our assigned duty is not for man's understanding, but to fulfill God's vision for our lives and the lives of those whom He wishes to lead into His divine will.

- They wrapped Jesus in swaddling clothes without knowing the value of His assignment and His Love to them. Likewise us, we are something wrapped in nothing when others don't recognize the assignment in us, through lack of understanding and Love. But, divine Love, Jesus' Love, through God's Love, understands the purpose of the assignment, and with His redeeming blood, knows the value, the greatness, and the dream that we have been born to tell the story that is, before the foundation of the world. Thus, His Divine Love has protected and also declares our assignment; by unwrapping us from nothing to something greater in Christ— the assignment to impact the world.

- God's Divine Love decreed our assignment—the assignment to impact the world for His Kingdom!

- Samson's full strength was not in his hair, but in the Love of God. It may be the belief that the strength was in Samson's hair, but God's presence in him was greater than the hair on his head. He was enslaved with chains–but he was given the chance to fulfill the purpose for which he was born...that is the power of Love. When it is all over, the Love of God conquers all.

Words of Wisdom

WORDS OF WISDOM ON LOVE AND PURITY

· Love purifies the hearts; for Love is always perfect, and perfect Love cannot be defiled.

· With the purity of Love, the heart is measured.

· Purity keeps the mind clear and prepares the heart for Love.

· The heart is the place where honesty dwells; a place of purity; a place where Love is nurtured, where deception is conquered and where darkness turns into light. When Love is present, it fills the emptiness within, leaving no place for unwanted indulgence.

WORDS OF WISDOM ON LOVE AND SHEPHERDING....

"A heart that is dedicated to the Love of God will always exhibit a conduct that is inspired by the Lord. A loving shepherd speaks and behaves in the manner that is conducive to the Love of God; thus he creates a platform from which he can effectively portray the message of Christ to others."

—Joseph M. Stowell

- Love is the key to all relationships; Love knows and under-stands what instruments must be used to defeat the spirit of hate. (David and Saul)

- If becoming a shepherd is important to us, then as leaders our behaviors should consistently reflect the Love of God in our lives; we should lead our flock with Love and gentleness of heart; our behavior should be the reflection of honesty both in our speech and in our conduct when dealing with others. Our speech and our behavior should be our hallmark of righ-teousness, of Love, of faith, and of purity.

- In order to exhibit unconditional Love, the Love must be of an unshakable faith in God.

- Love is at the heart of what it means to be a committed ser-vant of God.

- Divine Love flows and it is spotless; Love is sensitive to those who are broken; Love mends the broken heart.

- Without the Love of God, we are left defeated, angry and discouraged by life's journey. Love helps us to foster continued growth in our ministry, in which not only the children of God will be blessed, but it will also enhance our own testimony of Jesus' Love in our own lives.

- A shepherd's Love is a choice of commitment.

- The desire to become a shepherd is not so one may deliver the sheep to the slaughter, but to work on meeting their spiritual needs and, then to rely on the Holy Spirit to fill those sheep with the gift of the Holy Spirit by subduing their earthly de-sires. The shepherd's desire should not be seen as wanting to scatter and to destroy God's chosen ones.

- Seeing Love as a commitment over choice enables us to minister with our whole being to all mankind, even those whom we may consider not worthy of God's grace and mercy.

- It is important to remember that the Lord will not tolerate undesirable lifestyles among leaders; even though He Loves us with His divine Love, and even though He is gracious and merciful. Let us not forget that some of whom we may perceive to be the worst of sinners, because they may not suit our expectations, are the ones that we must be more sensitive to their needs, as this is the will of the Lord. True Love looks beyond the faults of others and seeks ways in which we are able to meet their needs, so that they too can enjoy the blessedness of salvation. We are commanded to Love even those who we do not like.

- Seeing the ministry as our own programs, as our own kingdom, and as an advancement and affirmation of ourselves will defeat the purpose for which we are called. Those attributes will only destroy our souls and rob us of our salvation.

- Loving others is a matter of godly commitment.

- Divine Love responds to the needs of others; a loving heart checks its resources wisely, as it prepares to meet the needs of others.

- Paul taught the church at Philippi to:

"Do nothing from selfishness or empty conceit, but with humility of mind, let each of us regard one another as more important than yourselves…"

—Philippians 2:3, NASB

- Godly Love knows its true assignment: 'I have come that they might have life…'

- The act of that Love states: 'We shall Love the Lord...' Motivated by a grateful response to Him.

- The act of the New Testament Love, the *agape* Love, is expressed when yielding ourselves to the Lord.

- We can understand Love as it is the key to the engine of the heart, knowing that as Love increases, hatred vanishes.

- Love is the example of truth; as the wise men knew that every child is born for a purpose, but when Christ was born, His birth was an emblem of truth and purpose.
- When you see your assignments appear in swaddling clothes of Love, then you will understand that you have had an encounter with divine Love, who is Christ Jesus.

- Divine Love searches for the lost sheep; it searches for the lost coin; and it searches for the lost son, and divine love rejoices when they are found.

A WORD OF ADMONITION ON THE POLLEN OF LOVE TO ALL

Not every bird or insect that pecks on the flowers of a fruit-bearing tree or plant endangers the fruits or the growth of the tree. The bird or bee helps the plants by carrying pollen to another tree or plant, something the tree cannot do for itself.. This principle demonstrated by the bird or bee is a primitive lesson on Love. Like the plant, we cannot live in self-centred ways if we want to bear fruit. We cannot fear mutual dependence. Leaders who accept their need for God and others will strengthen the platform from which they minister, allowing it to become fruitful and productive

The Anointing Exposes the Deeds of The Flesh, will open your eyes and expand your knowledge to the "Anointing in comparison to the deeds of the flesh, Jezebel Spirit, Ahab, and Lucifer." This book goes in-depth for readers who are desirous to grow spiritually through the different Scriptures on the anointing.

Available now in bookstores and online: ISBN 978-1-4497-1220-4

**For more information visit www.Meritshenry.org
or westbowpress.com**

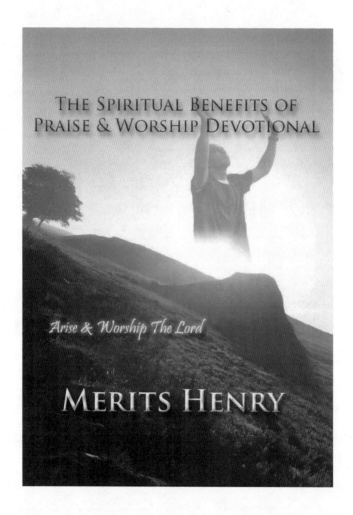

With an emphasis on the spiritual benefits of praise and worship, Merits seeks to leave you with an enduring sense of God's presence.

Available at www.Meritshenry.org

For more information visit www. Meritshenry.org